"To design is much more than simply to assemble, to order, or even to edit: it is to add value and meaning, to illuminate, to simplify, to clarify, to modify, to dignify, to dramatize, to persuade, and perhaps even to amuse. To design is to transform prose into poetry." —PAUL RAND

Hoaki Books, S.L.
C/ Ausiàs March, 128
08013 Barcelona, Spain
T. 0034 935 952 283
F. 0034 932 654 883
info@hoakibooks.com
www.hoaki.com

Design, Create, Thrill.
The Power of Graphic Design to Spark Emotions

ISBN: 978-84-17656-02-7
D.L.: B 12232-2019

Printed in Turkey

© Sara Caldas, 2020
© ELISAVA Barcelona School of Design and Engineering
© 2020 Hoaki Books, S.L.

Foreword: Albert Fuster, Academic Director, Elisava
Text revised by Tom Corkett
Book design: spread: David Lorente - Tomoko Sakamoto

Foreword

Design, Create, Thrill proposes a particular approach to the popular but sometimes misunderstood field that is graphic design. In this book, graphic design is presented as a dense, complex fabric of relations between human beings—a field in which there are intense interactions between people and designers, in either direction, with the aim of appealing not only to people's intelligence but also to their fears, goals and feelings. The author, Sara Caldas, embraces a wider understanding of the "emotional turn" opened up by Donald Norman to consider the emotional implications of design and their impact on human beings. Eschewing the scientific and sometimes cold interpretation of communication as a combination of text and image that constructs a message to connect a speaker and a listener in via a particular medium, the book delves into the breach opened up by emotions in the designed world.

To do so, Sara offers us different examples drawn from a wide range of areas, from games to packaging, from advertising to manifestoes, and from publishing to interaction design. The precise and convincing examples presented allow graphic design to be treated here as a key element that simultaneously builds and helps us to understand the overwhelming quantity of images and information that we are exposed to daily and that we tend to describe as "visual culture." In the book, pictures, colours, typographies, hierarchies and points of view become key elements that appeal to the context and people's backgrounds, at the same time as they define our mindset. And as a result, graphic design becomes something stronger than a simple tool in the hands of capitalist consumerism: it emerges as a central medium for raising awareness and asking human beings to take a position on social, political and environmental issues.

But dealing with emotions also means dealing with a feeling subject. And here the extreme care taken by Sara to set out and explain issues that are commonly underestimated in graphic design books becomes relevant. By bringing to the fore the importance of materiality, volume, space, texture and depth, the author draws attention to a plethora of new elements that add layers of complexity to the design object. Design products become devices that appeal not only to the linguistic mind, or to the observer's eye, but to a whole body that interacts with an environment that graphic design is also part of. Valuing the processes and means of elements commonly hidden behind the raw visual shape helps us to reflect on the actions of designers and on the reception of an active and critically built audience.

By going to such lengths to investigate, explain and connect so many references, the book reveals how graphic design is not merely a consequential technique applied to a previously existing idea, but a discipline that is capable of building content and even meaning. It is a major medium with clear importance as a field of knowledge and as a path to understanding our interactions with one another, our relationship with our environment and our own existence.

Enjoy the book—and feel it, too.

Albert Fuster, PhD Academic Director, Elisava

Emotions

What are emotions? This is the question I asked myself before I began this project. Generally, people understand the concept of emotion, but coming up with a solid definition for it seems to be a more difficult matter. It is difficult to explain something as immaterial as an emotion. That's why I found it necessary to clarify its meaning: I wanted to have a clearer insight into what makes people emote. Etymologically, *emotion* comes from the Latin *emovere*, which conveys the idea of moving out or getting out of oneself. From this we may deduce that it is possible that when people get emotional, they in some way exteriorize their emotions. They do so through their voices or body motions, including facial expressions and movements.[1]

Emotions are the reason why we cry at the movies, connect with others, get mad, laugh, and do many other things besides. But does anyone ever stop to think about why we do these things? Do we know what we are feeling? Do we realise we are feeling emotions? We are so used to our emotions that we don't actually process them as a rational behaviour. We perceive our emotional reactions as a natural instinct to what has an impact on us—a sort of extra layer that goes on top of our basic survival instincts and provides meaning in our lives.

1 — ESAD. (n.d.). Psicologia das Emoções. Retrieved (March 22, 2015) from: http://web.esad.ip-leiria.pt/PDMIII/3080031/site-grupo/investigacao/neuropsi-cologia.html

However, emotions play a bigger role in our existence. In fact, they are not only the reason why we feel what we feel but also the motivation behind what we do and what we think on a daily basis. If we consider the fact that they work at the subconscious level of our brains, it becomes clear that emotions are a significant part of human survival. They are patterns that guide us toward correct behaviours and help us to avoid bad and dangerous ones. They also help us to make all kinds of decisions that we face throughout the day, whether we are booking an appointment or buying one brand's product instead of that of another.

According to the famous neurobiologist António Damásio, emotions and all related feelings are responsible—or partially responsible in conjunction with other mechanisms linked to reasoning—for the tasks and actions that we perform. They help us to make predictions, plan future actions in light of said predictions and participate in cognitive and communicative functions. All these acts are highly relevant to this book's framework. The results of Damásio's research led him to conclude that emotions are important when people make decisions. When we face a situation in which we need to make a choice—which continuously happens throughout the day—it is necessary to have knowledge of the situation, be aware of the different options before us and consider the immediate and future consequences of each choice. A rigorous analysis of every hypothesis would take too long, and so either the chosen option would no longer be opportune or people would get lost in their mental lists of pros and cons. As Damásio puts it, "Uncontrolled or misdirected emotion can be a major source of irrational behaviour."[2] Damásio's investigations have had significant repercussions on our knowledge of emotions and on ideas about the interdependency between emotion and reason. In his book *Descartes' Error*, he argues that these two dimensions are connected and that any attempt to separate leads to our misunderstanding human beings' behaviours, attitudes, skills and decisions. In fact, pure reason does not exist: we think with our rationality and our emotions simultaneously.

Damásio theorized that emotions work with rationality on an auxiliary basis and actually influence some of the most important cognitive

2 — Damásio, A. R. (1995). *Descartes' Error: Emotion, Reason, and the Human Brain.* New York: Avon Books.

processes required for human survival. Viewed from this perspective, the intrinsic relationship between decision making and emotion seems obvious. Decisions are not emotionally neutral but call on the individual's subjective, underlying emotions, which trigger the action that he or she takes. Every human being has an inventory of fundamental and universal emotions that serve as a basis for action. The older and more experienced we get, the more complex and particular these emotions become, and eventually they define each one of us as individuals. A simple event—whether it be an external one or something internal such as a thought—is all it takes for a person to experience some kind of emotional response. However, this response is not dependent on the event itself, but rather on the way each person appraises it. The same event can trigger totally different responses in different people. This is known as emotional competence, and it is described by Rafael Bisquerra in his book *Universo de emociones* (*Universe of Emotions*) as "the set of knowledge, skills, abilities and attitudes necessary to become aware of, understand, express and regulate emotional phenomena appropriately."[3]

Further on in his book, Bisquerra argues that each of us should be responsible for our own emotional intelligence. Each one of us should try

3 — Bisquerra, R. (2015). *Universo de emociones* (2nd ed.). Valencia: PalauGea.

to understand our own emotions and become aware of what we respond to and why we do so. The objective here is to prevent impulsive behaviours and manage the balance between negative and positive emotions, which will benefit our well-being and that of others. To understand our emotional repertoire, we have to experience its full range and enhance the aspects of it that make us feel better. This is why art plays an important role in our lives. It has the ability to spark emotions, and although these are not real in the sense that they are the stimulated through aesthetics rather than through biographical events, we are able to express them and share them with others. Eventually, some creative professionals realized that art's ability to stimulate a great range of emotions could also be applied to design projects in order to create deeper connections between the user and the product. And so the concept of *emotional design* started being used in design practices decide to create the book that you now have in your hands.

This book is the result of the research work that I carried out while I was completing my master's degree in communication design at Elisava, a design and engineering school in Barcelona. At the time when I was performing that work, I reached the conclusion that a book would be the best way to represent and share my findings, and that insight quickly evolved into something that the school and I thought would be worth sharing with a wider audience.

Emotions applied to design

"To design is much more than simply to assemble, to order, or even to edit: it is to add value and meaning, to illuminate, to simplify, to clarify, to modify, to dignify, to dramatize, to persuade, and perhaps even to amuse. To design is to transform prose into poetry."[4] —PAUL RAND

4 — Rand, P. (1993). *Design, Form, and Chaos*. New Haven: Yale University Press.

A design should help people relate to its concept so that their experience of it is a satisfactory and memorable one. Therefore, designs should not only be logically and viably structured but also be the product of a sound understanding of which elements are required to create an emotional bond between the designed item and its user.

The concept of emotional design is still unknown to some people, though it is simple to figure out the broad strokes of it. When asked about what the term means, some people told me they think it's design's ability to spark emotions—ones that the public feels because of the memories the design evokes, the aesthetic mood it transmits or the symbolism it represents. Others consider emotional design to be a more "human" and personalized form of design that inspires empathy within people. It is a way of designing that reflects on the crucial role emotions play in the human ability to understand the world, and things designed based on this approach promise to enhance the quality of life of their users. A successful emotion-driven design improves the relationship between the audience and the "product," creating deep emotional bonds between the two.

An object capable of exteriorizing some kind of emotion brings the "I don't know why, but I want it" feeling that all of us may have experienced at least once in our lives. The emotion could be conveyed by just a simple element that fulfils a need—even if there is no scientific or technical explanation as to why it does so—and thereby gives purpose to the object's purchase. If we look around, the things we surround ourselves with reflect choices we have made to achieve emotional outcomes. Some of our belongings reflect how particular objects affect our mood—they can make us feel excited, amused, happy or confident—and these emotional benefits are ultimately the reason behind our having acquired them. Design can play a crucial role in defining a product's emotional benefits. By manipulating the appearance, usability and intellectualization of a product, designers can shape the emotional influence it has on the user and, therefore, encourage meaningful relationships. Don Norman, a member of the Nielsen Norman group—a user experience and usability consulting firm—suggests that there are three aspects of design and that each of them induces emotions at different levels. He labels calls aspects *visceral*, *behavioural* and *reflective* design.[5]

Visceral design works at the deepest and most primitive part of our brain: the reptilian brain. This part of the brain is in charge of the immediate

5 — Norman, D. A. (2004). *Emotional Design: Why We Love (or Hate) Everyday Things.* New York: Basic Books.

responses needed for survival, awareness of the present moment, analysis of the stimuli perceived by our senses and decisions on the appropriate way to behave in response to those stimuli.[6] Viscerally designed objects therefore elicit an immediate and positive response from the user. They are all about appearance and first impressions, and the visual impact that this kind of design has on the user is certainly its most important aspect.

6 — Barco, B. (2014). "El Cerebro Narrativo," in *El Cerebro Narrativo* (pp. 1–18). Barcelona.

If we shift our focus a little further along the emotional spectrum, we get to behavioural design, which is related to the usability of a product. In other words, a behaviourally designed object is one that immensely enhances the experience of the user who interacts with it. Ideally, the aim is for the final product to provide a seamless experience via functions that are clear, simple and easily recognizable. Even more importantly, the user's interaction with the product should be pleasurable. The better the physical feeling, the higher the quality of the user experience.

The third level of design that Norman proposes is reflective design, and this is where "the highest levels of feeling, emotions, and cognition reside."[7] At this level, the user's interpretation of and insights about the product acquire greater relevance. From another point of view, reflective design is also about self-image and the message a product sends to others regarding its owner. Some decisions that people make when they purchase a product—for example, "I won't buy this because it wouldn't seem appropriate to my age" or "I'll buy this because it will make me look funnier/smarter/ more adult"—are made at the reflective level and are properties of reflective processing. The more consumers associate the product with prestige, rarity and exclusiveness, the more they will appreciate it. Therefore, the reflective aspect of an object cannot be determined by anyone except the person who owns it or is contemplating it. A design does not need to be perfectly made to provoke reflection; what matters are the stories that the beholder builds around it and the memories that it evokes, which work as powerful triggers of long-lasting emotions. Although Norman describes these three levels as having a separate existence from one another, he stresses that any product should aim to contain all three of them. A rich emotional bond between a product and its user is only possible if the user engages with it on all these levels. A product must be attractive, pleasurable, effective and understandable, and in attempting to give it these attributes, the designer must aim to achieve a balance between all three levels of design. If he or she does this successfully, the product will attract customers who will develop a lifelong loyalty to it.

7 — Norman, *op. cit.*, 38.

Emotional graphic design

"Graphic design is everywhere, touching everything we do, everything we see, everything we buy."[8] —FRANC NUNOO-QUARCOO

8 — Nunoo-Quarcoo, Franc (2003). *Paul Rand: Modernist Design*. New York: The Center for Art and Visual Culture.

Objects can be loved. They can be considered friends. They can understand our needs, wishes and feelings, and they can chart a path straight to our hearts. Several authors and designers have already demonstrated how emotion-driven design can be more effective in connecting with the public compared to traditional design approaches. However, the studies and theories that have done so are all focused specifically on product design, industrial design or Web design. In fact, graphic design is only mentioned in them as a discrete component of a given product that could also help it to convey emotion. Yet doesn't graphic design also create emotional connections with the public? Can it not be beautifully appealing, easy to understand and capable of bringing out the viewer's innermost memories? I believe that all this is possible. Otherwise, why is it that sometimes people steal posters—for example, advertisements for concerts or new albums by iconic musicians—from public spaces within a few days or hours of their being put up? Why are some products bought only because of their packaging? And why are books often judged by their covers? The answer is simple: all of these examples involve emotional graphic design that creates deep bonds between people and product.

The writer Grassa Toro, in his book about the celebrated Spanish illustrator and graphic designer Isidro Ferrer, describes what happens to design pieces once they leave the designer's studio and are consumed by people. In my view, his take on this "consumption" explains the importance of designing based on an emotional perspective: "Doesn't the basis of the designer's work involve 'producing effects on a third party'? Yes, it does, this work, poster, label, brochure, cover, card, book, animation, which are released from their creator when they become public, are, for this very reason, open to the free interpretation of every human being, to their free acceptance, rejection, enjoyment or suffering, and will become poetry once again under new gaze of that unknown individual."[9]

Graphic design is usually the "front cover" of any product, service or company, as it is the first thing users have contact with. For this reason, I believe it should carry emotional value in itself.

9 — Toro, G. (2003). *Isidro Ferrer: Al pan, pan, y al vino, pan.* (BCD Foundation & Ministry of Science and Technology, Eds.) (122/250). Barcelona.

When it does, the sentiments that the design conveys have an immediate impact on people, resulting in an improved relationship between them and the product. Design aspects play a crucial role in earning customers' acceptance and in developing a brand identity, and this creates the need to consider the consumer's expectations and emotionally connect with them. Moreover, the increasingly saturated nature of many markets for products and services makes it essential to create a visual identity that is capable of connecting with the target audience in order to add emotional and life-quality values to that relationship. Only in this way is it possible for a product or brand to distinguish itself from its competitors. In an era when visual communication seems to be the core ingredient of exchanging messages and ideas with the world around us, we find ourselves in a state of "continuous partial attention"[10] because visual works are constantly fighting to make us focus on them. As a result of this, designers should direct their communication strategies toward designing emotionally relevant pieces that people enjoy having around and that are easier to pay attention to. After all, information is processed more deeply and better remembered if it creates an emotional link.

Of no less importance is creating a design that makes people think in a way that encourages them to recognize themselves in that design. I believe that it is necessary to incorporate an intellectual dimension into graphic design projects by using real emotions to communicate a message. Ultimately, it is our task as graphic designers to harmonize concepts, thoughts and ideas with the goal of touching someone's heart. To this end, it is crucial to design with the hopes, fears, dreams, feelings and self-image of the audience in mind. The ultimate goal of an emotional design is to promise enhanced quality of life and a better society for all.

10 — Stone, L. (1998). "Continuous Partial Attention." Retrieved from: https://lindastone.net/qa/continuous-partial-attention/

About the project

"Great designs, like great art and literature, can break the rules and survive forever, but only a few are gifted enough to be great."[11]
—DONALD A. NORMAN

11 — Norman, *op. cit.*, 67.

The world needs more graphic design that is great, that can survive longer, and that can create deeper relationships with society. I believe emotion-driven design is the path that can lead us to this goal. Emotions play a crucial role in humans' ability to understand the world, and so an emotionally focused graphic communication should be prioritized by the graphic design community. Unfortunately, as I have previously mentioned, people aren't always aware of the power that emotions carry, or of how to use and control them for a greater good. In my opinion, creatives should understand the causes and consequences of them, evaluate their intensity and recognize and use the language of emotions in their work. Moreover, mapping humanity's huge range of emotions is a key step that will make it possible to clearly identify which emotion it is desirable to elicit in a given situation.

My starting point when I decided to write this book was to study and analyse the frameworks and theories about emotional design, most of which relate to product and industrial design. My intention was to find all the different ways in which designers could use emotions in their work and understand how they could be adapted and implemented into the graphic design world. In my view, graphic design has never been as valued by society as it is today. This gives we designers the opportunity to responsibly use our work to make a difference and to encourage meaningful relationships between designer and audience, design piece and viewer, and so on. It is time to break from the mainstream approach and start offering a stimulating and emotional graphic experience.

In creating this book, I wanted to raise designers' and creatives' awareness of how important emotions are to the success of a design. We possess the skills and tools to capture the emotional climate of a given context and enhance it to foster credibility and trust. Emotion-driven design can motivate and engage people at an entirely different level, as well as lead them in the right direction. By equipping ourselves with all the different possible techniques for making a design emotional, we broaden the range of possibilities for combining images, shapes, contrasts, colours, materials and information. For this reason, my hope is that this book will help me and other designers to start profound and empathetic conversations with our audiences—and consequently, to get to know them, their values and their lifestyles better—and that it will motivate us to grow into professionals who create well-thought-out designs that contribute to a better world.

The structure of this book

"Go further: recognize the interdependence, power, and influence of your role as a professional, and let it resonate with the world around you."[12] —DAVID B. BERMAN

12 — Berman, D. B. (2009). *Do Good Design. How Designers Can Change the World*. (M. Nolan, M. S. Anderson, R. Berman, & S. Lysnes, Eds.) (1st ed.). Berkeley: New Riders.

Design, Create, Thrill may be seen as a guide to "go further." Its aim is to help the design community to fill its work with emotions and, consequently, to make its audience emote. The book presents twenty-three principles which bring the designer closer to an emotion-driven design.

These principles are grouped into chapters according to the level of emotions that they elicit, starting with principles that may be seen as the surface level of our emotional strata. These provoke a visceral response, produced subconsciously in our brain as a result of evolutionary processes. From the first chapters onwards, the goal is to dig into the subject of emotions in design a little deeper, working on each layer of the emotional universe. During this journey, the reader will find principles that elicit long-lasting emotions within the viewers, bringing out feelings of connectedness between the latter and the creators.

Toward the end of the book, the designer's own emotions are taken into consideration to a greater degree, and the reader will be shown what can be achieved when a true and unique passion for the craft is channelled into work projects.

To better explain these concepts and analyse how they may be applied to real design projects, each principle is associated with two designers, design studios and/or projects that illustrate the related concept. The reader will find timeless design pieces from all over the world and from distinct points in time. Throughout the book, I emphasize that although emotional graphic design per se is not something commonly heard about, emotions are inherently human and have always been present in the minds of great designers, even if only at a subconscious level. I cannot objectively state that these examples aren't influenced by my own personal tastes; they are. Emotions are a subjective concept, so it is only natural that this very selection is representative of the things that personally affect me, that make me emotional. That subjectivity should nevertheless not detract from the excellence of the selected examples. In this book itself, these example works will be clearly connected to one of the specific principles that guide the narrative, but that does not mean that they exclusively produce emotions at the level focused on in the chapter; they will in fact be connected with a multitude of other principles as well. Each one of these projects is a case in point of how commitment to the profession and affection for the target audience can yield outstanding and emotionally intricate results.

Throughout the book, the reader will also find brief interviews and conversations with some of the creators and designers of the example works. The aim here is to provide the reader with insights into the creative thinking of these designers and how they incorporate emotional design theories into their activity.

Ultimately, this book is meant to be used as a tool to create successful emotion-driven design and to help designers to harmonize concepts, thoughts and ideas to *touch* someone's heart (even if it is just their own). My humble hope is that this book encourages readers to design with emotions, for emotions.

Disclaimer

This book is not a secret recipe for emotional graphic design. It intends to point out various creators' and designers' perspectives on how to successfully attach a more profound meaning to a graphic designer's output—an emotional layer that is able to establish a deeper connection with the end user. Given the subjective nature of this topic, it will always be difficult to draw up a clear step-by-step guide on how to create this emotional layer. This does not mean that such a task is impossible or that the path that I trace here is the only one possible. I invite readers to engage with the work with this point in mind. It is meant as a source of inspiration and not as the ultimate guide to producing emotional graphic design.

Part of what makes designing for emotion difficult is that emotions are personal and temporary and only intelligible if the person who is experiencing them is also taken into account.[13] That is, being aware of a design's social and cultural context is of particular importance. The audience's concerns, personal experiences and emotional states affect their interpretation of the design. This influences the emotional responses that the design provokes, and these responses can be difficult to predict and explain. What we as creative minds face if we embrace emotional design is the rather difficult challenge of understanding how to cause shifts in emotion and how to influence emotional responses to our designs.

13 — Desmet, P. (2002). *Designing Emotions*. Delft; Delft University of Technology.

My wish is that the readers will take these principles as food for thought and as ideas and challenges that we can introduce into our work to break away from a lifeless and mundane type of graphic design. Hard work, experimentation and a journey into our own emotional universe will bring us as designers closer to the fundamental goal of graphic design: creating something truly memorable.

Due to the primitive essence of our existence, bright colours as well as round and symmetrical shapes appeal to us on a subconscious level. Moreover, humans are intrinsically communicative, and so we perceive personality traits in some design pieces and enjoy engaging with these at a multisensorial level, exploring all that the design can offer. Nevertheless, information should never be too hidden so as not to cause frustration in viewers.

Appealingness

Hey Studio: "Commentary – Berlin Exhibition", 2015. Flag (detail)

"Design awakens all the senses."
—LEE KUN-HEE

Attraction

Nature has always provided inspiration for art and design, in part because of its attractive shapes and colours. Since the beginning of humankind, we have evolved to coexist in an environment alongside other human beings, animals, plants and natural elements.

One facet of the evolutionary process is that males and females of the same species evolved to look attractive to each other, ensuring the continuity of the species. Similarly, flowers have evolved to look attractive to birds and bees in order to better spread their pollen, and fruits have evolved to be attractive to primates and other animals so they could easily spread their seeds. These evolutionary processes explain why most flowers and fruits are colourful, rounded and smooth, with fragrant tastes and smells. Throughout time, not only have plants developed in order to attract animals and people, but those same animals have also changed to become attracted to these plants.[14]

14 — Norman, *op.cit.*

Most likely, the human love for bright, highly saturated colours and rounded shapes derives from this mutual dependence between people and plants and its consequent coevolution process. Because these processes happened at a primitive level, these preferences and instincts are consistent across people and cultures.

With this is mind, it is likely that design pieces that are able to capture the bright colours, high contrast and organic shapes present in nature will generate pleasure and create interest among the public. Moreover, designs that are aesthetically more attractive to viewers can be perceived as more reliable, intelligent, credible and persuasive.[15]

15 — van Gorp, T., & Adams, E. (2012). *Design for Emotion*. (Meg Dunkerley & Heather Scherer, Eds.). Waltham: Elsevier.

Throughout history, many designers have used this principle in their approaches to communication. Soviet propaganda and recruitment posters, for example, made use of highly saturated reds to raise viewers' state of arousal in an attempt to motivate them to beat the enemy. On the other side of the world, Milton Glaser and other contemporaneous American graphic designers developed pieces with high chromatic intensity and solid masses of colour that are still appreciated today.

Creating designs that capture the 1960s and 1970s American graphic design feel is one of the goals of the Barcelona-based Hey Studio. It achieves this goal by applying clean shapes, a lively colour palette and bold graphics to its designs. This small studio focuses its work on brand identity, editorial design and illustration, and its colourful and geometric approach to design

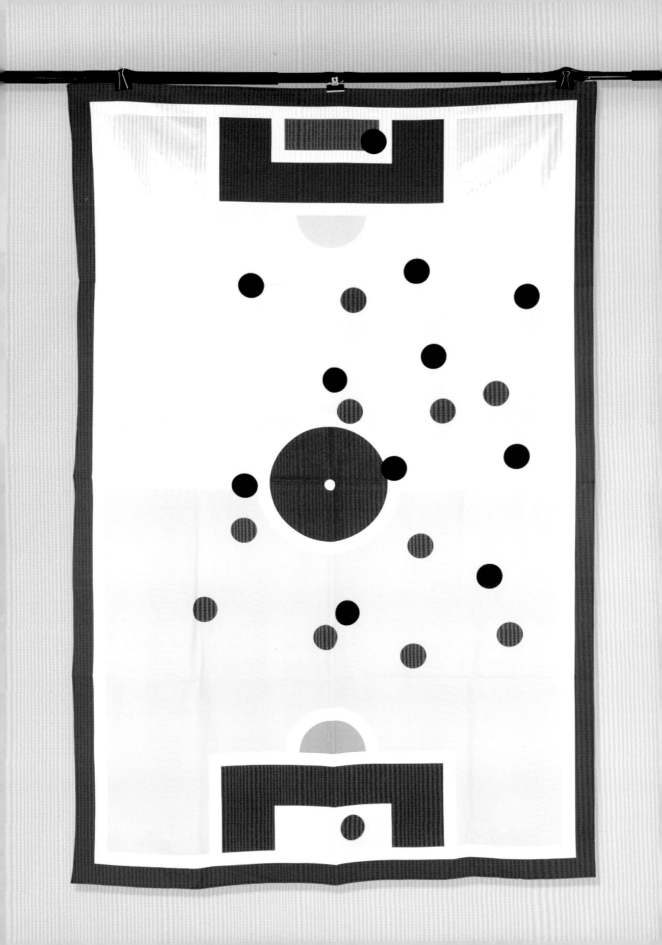

has taken it beyond a local Spanish clientele and brought it to the attention of companies like Apple, Vodafone, the *Wall Street Journal* and *Monocle*.

When asked about the reasons behind its hued and powerful graphic style, Verònica Fuerte, Hey Studio's founder, says that "it's not just a style, it's an attitude. It's something open, fresh and simple with a strong idea behind it, and very bold graphics. I believe design is for everyone, not just a specific target, so that's why it's so direct and fresh."[16]

People are attracted to such graphic choices, and we can see this in action if we look at the website of Hey Studio, which features all of the studio's projects in small tiles. One instantly spots the bright palettes that it uses across its portfolio. This not only sends a very positive message to the audience but also creates a fresh and energetic feel that is likely to be pleasing to most viewers. "Colours are emotions. Yellow and black are not the same; every colour spreads its own message. Then, of course, the more colours you use, the more emotions the design will elicit," says Verónica. "Our work might emote a great mass of people because colour communicates a lot of things, a lot of sensations. And yes, it might be more visually appealing than other projects that are more muted. The thing is, colour attracts!"

16 — Gosling, E. (2017, March). "Hey Studio founder Verònica Fuerte on the importance of self-initiated projects and how to survive a crisis," in *Creative Boom*. Retrieved from: https://www.creativeboom.com/features/hey-studio/

The same American graphical influence that we see in Hey Studio's portfolio also inspired the Portuguese graphic designer João Machado. Undoubtedly, his work, which mainly comprises posters, fits in the category of attractive emotional graphic design due to its bright colours, playful arrangement of geometric and rounded shapes, and bold contrasts between flat surfaces and textured patterns. We can also spot influences from Portuguese popular art, comic books and Nordic modernism in Machado's graphic assets, elements that make his posters invitations to contemplate and admire. Some critics believe that his works "depart from their practical function of communicating events, to communicate the design of the poster as an event in itself and, therefore, as an aesthetic event."[17]

João Machado's success came about at a moment when graphic design in Portugal was still trying to prove itself as a discipline that could motivate viewers and effectively convey a specific message. Regardless of his international accomplishments, Machado helped to define graphic design as a profession in Portugal, giving it a new and fresh importance nationally. People began to

17 — Providência, F., Bártolo, J., & Silva, H. S. (2016). *João Machado - 1/ Colecção Designers Portugueses*. (José Bártolo, Ed.) (1st ed.). Matosinhos: Cardume Editores.

Verónica Fuerte

Graphic designer, founder of Hey Studio

The first thing I notice about Hey Studio's work is the abundance of colours. In looking at your webpage, one immediately sees the bright and highly saturated palette you use across your projects. Why is colour such an important feature in your work?

I founded the studio in 2007, but colour has always been important for me since I was a student and even since I was a child. That is why I decided to study graphic design: because we had a class that was only about colour. For me, colour is at the same level as typography, photography and illustration. It is another element with which you can design. It is a way to explore a design project. Of course a project is not only made of colour but is rather the sum of other elements. However, colour is emotion and through it we can communicate a lot of different things; that is why it is so important.

How do you choose the colour palette for each project?

We don't have a formula. A lot of times we pick the palette according to sensations and emotions. But we never forget the theory that comes with the brief. A project aimed at people who are 20/30/40 years old twenty, thirty or forty is very different to one aimed at an audience of people who are in their sixties. And one for a technological company will not be the same as one for a fashion brand. Because everything we create answers to a brief, we spend a lot of time working on the colour palette. We try many new colours to finally pick the ones that best suit the project.

What does emotional design mean for you?

The way I see it, emotional design has two perspectives. First, there's the point of view of the project, the designer himself —there is always a personal and emotional essence within a project. Obviously, a project must follow a list of values, but if it doesn't create emotions, it doesn't work. On the other hand, there's the point of view of the client, the public, the audience and the way they perceive those emotions. To summarize, emotional design encompasses both the point of view of the designer—from the inside—and how the public or client receives the design. You have to thrill them, surprise them!

(left) João Machado: "Construir Bauen," 2001. Poster / (right) João Machado: "Oceanos," 1998. Poster

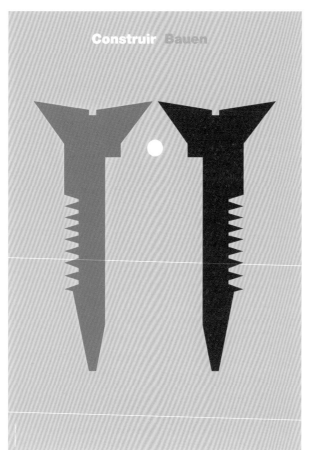

Construir Bauen

OCEANOS

cinanima

29º Festival
Internacional
de Cinema
de Animação

07
13
Nov.
05

ESPINHO
PORTUGAL

ORGANIZAÇÃO
NASCENTE - COOPERATIVA DE ACÇÃO CULTURAL, CRL. / CÂMARA MUNICIPAL DE ESPINHO

MC
(Ministério da Cultura)   ICAM

appreciate his posters and flyers, which were suddenly seen as seductive and interesting pieces of communication. From his multiple posters for the animation film festival Cinanima to his pieces focused on social and environmental communication, João Machado has displayed a remarkable plasticity and a mastery of colour combination, creating compositions of great contemporaneity, seductiveness and appeal.

Besides our instinctive attraction to highly saturated colours, colour itself can also appeal to us in different ways. Studies reveal that there are some colours that humans may perceive as safe and relaxing—like those found on the blue and green spectrum—whereas red, yellow and orange are considered more dynamic, aggressive and active, eliciting excitement or fear.[18] Either way, both form and colour, if properly used, can have a strong emotional effect on viewers and instantly grab their attention. It is therefore the designer's job to match the "looks" with the "feelings" and to provide a graphic piece that is both visually and conceptually attractive.

In short, nature can be a good place to find a wide range of impactful visual solutions.

18 — W. Jordan, P. (2000). *Designing Pleasurable Products* (2nd ed.). Oxon: Taylor & Francis.

Symmetry

The evolutionary and biological aspects that I mentioned in the previous statement can also explain humans' relationship with symmetry. Darwin's theory of natural selection also operates at the level of procreation: certain members within a given species are selected as sexual partners by its other members. This selection occurs due to particular qualities and characteristics that will secure stronger descendants and the continuity of the species. Within humans, one of these characteristics was symmetry of faces and bodies—an asymmetry could mean a genetic deficiency. What we now consider to be a beautiful face tends to be more symmetrical than one that doesn't attract our attention as much; this attraction stems from our ancestors' choice of the fittest.

Providing another perspective on symmetry, the physicist Alan Lightman states in an essay published in *Orion Magazine* that it "represents order, and we crave order in this strange universe we find ourselves in. The search for symmetry, and the emotional pleasure we derive when we find it, must help us make sense of the world around us, just as we find satisfaction in the repetition of the seasons and the reliability of friendships. Symmetry is also economy. Symmetry is simplicity. Symmetry is elegance."[19]

Most likely, this is why we feel predisposed to find symmetrical shapes and designs appealing, and why we feel comfortable and relaxed when looking at them. Symmetry means that we only have to understand one side of the object; the other side is just its reflection. The more easily we process a design, the more positive our aesthetic response will be.

19 — Lightman, A. (2013, March/April). "The Symmetrical Universe," in *Orion Magazine*. Retrieved from: http://us2.campaign-archive2.com/?u=1854296747731744c923a33ef&id=cbe7bed4f0&buffer_share=997c7&utm_source=buffer

In the graphic design world, it is common to see symmetrical layouts that are also clean and aesthetically simple. I am particularly fond of some Japanese book cover designs. There is something alluring about their restrained use of graphic components and the careful choice of information presented. Within a compilation of book cover designs from East Asia, I read a quote from Jon Dowling—author of the book and partner at the multidisciplinary graphic design studio Leterme Dowling—with which I couldn't agree more: "What these covers have in common, regardless of their region, is a shared serenity and balance that resonates beautifully with their simple, uncluttered and modern aesthetic."[20]

One of the aspects that gives these covers such appealing symmetry is the harmony and balance of Japanese typographical characters.

20 — Dowling, J. (2016). *Book Cover Design from East Asia*. Ifold: Counter-Print.

Originating from Chinese calligraphy art, these characters evoke beauty, and they work almost as a pattern. With the evolution of typography, these characters became more sophisticated, and they were adapted by the countries that used them—China, Japan, South Korea and Vietnam. Nowadays, some Japanese designers—for example, The Simple Society, Asyl, Coton Design and Yuta Takahashi—create engaging book covers that seduce both the East and the West.

Don't get me wrong: symmetry doesn't mean that everything has to be minimalist and clean. The wings of a butterfly, for example, are not, and nor are snowflakes or flowers. And art and design works are certainly not always minimalist, as can be seen when one looks at decorative and ornamental art. The intricate patterns seen in ornamental book frames from the Renaissance are as symmetrical as the clean Japanese book covers on the following pages. And for that reason, they are equally appealing.

Inspired by this ornamental style, the work of the Canadian graphic artist Marian Bantjes is a feast for the eyes. Bantjes is known for her detailed vector art, her obsessive hand-rendered patterning, and her highly ornamental style. There is a feeling of symmetry in most of her works produced for books and magazines that soothes the viewer in what could

Yuta Takahashi: (top) Michael Debus: *Erkenntnisweg und Heiliger Geist*, 2017. Book design / (middle) Michael Debus: *Trinität* Special Edition, 2015. Book design / (bottom) Johannes Kühl, Johannes Greiner: *Anthroposophische Gesellschaft und Freie Hochschule für Geisteswissenschaft*, 2016. Book design

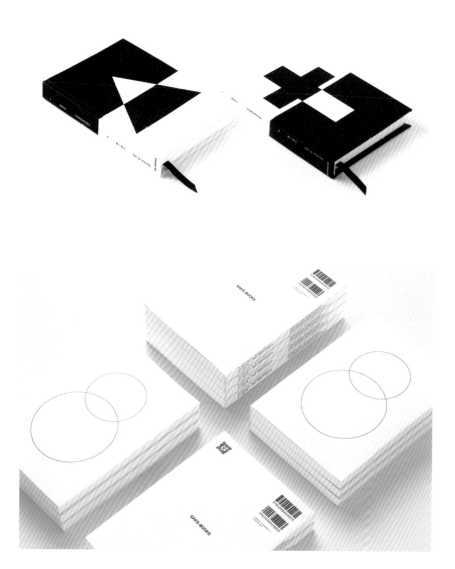

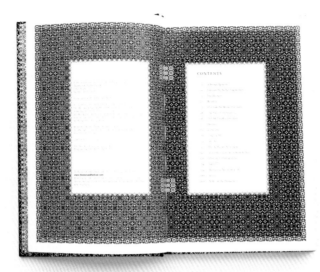

CONTENTS

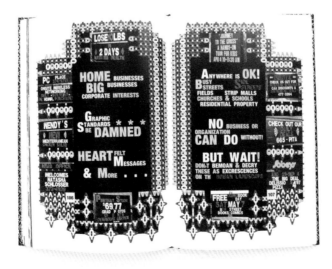

otherwise be a chaotic visual experience. As her friend and renowned graphic designer Stefan Sagmeister puts it, "Marian's work might be my favourite example of beauty facilitating the communication of meaning."[21] There is a good reason for turning to editorial pieces to exemplify this principle. A book is something that is symmetrical in itself, and thus designers may be motivated to produce equally symmetrical layouts to fill the blank pages. We could say Marian Bantjes follows this principle in *I Wonder*, a self-designed and self-illustrated book that actually makes the reader feel a sense of wonder. Each spread has a one-of-a-kind illustration—made from materials that range from flowers to pasta—that beautifully frames the artist's thoughts and contemplations. But these illustrations weren't made as mere decoration. Instead, they add important information that is tightly connected with the texts themselves. Bantjes uses symmetry with a particular purpose that adds value and meaning to the book. One of the many reviews of this project described it as a work that " rises above the usual design book in the way Bantjes marries her text with the shapes and patterns her imagination enters to reveal layers of meaning ."[22]

All things considered, it wouldn't be fair to the designers presented here to finish this section without clarifying that symmetry is not the only emotional quality of their pieces. Symmetry only elicits a superficial emotion that works for a short period of time. These books—especially *I Wonder*—make use of several different methods (which I will talk about through this book) that make them highly emotional pieces of graphic design. If you don't know where to start a creative project, try thinking about a symmetrical way to present the information and go from there.

21 — Bantjes, M. (2010). *I Wonder.* London: Thames & Hudson.

22 — Biederbeck, T. (2010). "Marian Bantjes Wonder Worth," in *Felt and Wire.*

Marian Bantjes: "I Wonder," 2010. Book design

‹

Human like

People often associate the message communicated by a piece of graphic design with certain characteristics with which they personally identify. Additionally, people tend to pay more attention to graphic communications that, from their point of view, reflect their own personalities. This tendency could imply that the more *human* the graphics are, the more exhilarating the relationship between the design and its viewers will be. They will see the design as a friend and not only as a visual message.

Introducing human features into graphic design is especially important when developing a graphic brand identity, as those traits will be immediately connected with the brand. Clients that are firms or big corporations might find it scary to opt for the personality-as-a-design approach. However, this approach not only makes them seem honest and open about their brands but also attracts customers who trust and appreciate honesty.

Notably, the New York City-based start-up Zocdoc, which provides online tools for finding a doctor and booking medical appointments, did exactly that. With the help of the agency Wolff Olins NY, Zocdoc rebranded itself to appear more friendly and empathetic to its users.

In addition to moving its branding's colour scheme away from a palette of blue and green, which is often associated with the graphic identity of health companies, Zocdoc also humanized this sector by creating a logo/mascot that focuses on the patient rather than the doctor. The new logo obtains its emotional appeal through a combination of elements that resemble facial expressions that convey how a patient might be feeling. Zee, the name given to the logo, is created out of the letter Z, with two dots for the eyes and the foot of the letter for the mouth. In its usual position, Zee salutes us with a warm smile that we are predisposed—through our mirror neurons—to return. This design gives patients the confidence that Zocdoc will take good care of them and understands what they are going through. In fact, the start-up's VP of marketing, Richard Fine, defines the rebrand as "the way healthcare should look—friendly, simple, and most of all, reflective of patients and real life."[23]

It is part of humans' biological background to be social creatures who are prepared to interact with the world. Additionally, there is a psychological phenomenon that causes people to see patterns in random stimuli. This phenomenon is called *pareidolia*, and it is why we tend to read emotional responses and facial expressions into all kinds of moving

23 — Wolff Olins. (2016). "Zocdoc." Retrieved (February 5, 2017) from: https://www.wolffolins.com/case-studies/zocdoc/

Wolff Olins: "Zocdoc," 2016. Corporate identity

⟩

and static objects. This phenomenon leads to the anthropomorphizing of the nonliving things with which we have contact in our daily lives, making us interact with them in the same way as we would interact with another person.

Facial expressions can therefore be found in or simply added to many ordinary objects, and this trick can be used for communication purposes. Colours, materials and finishings also have an influence on the way in which we interpret expressions. Isidro Ferrer, one of the most famous Spanish graphic designers today, creates characters from various objects and textures that appear to be looking at us and telling us a story that reveals the information that the piece was commissioned to communicate. Ferrer says that he likes "to find faces hidden in a wooden block, the faces revealed in a seal, in a coin"[24] and then to use them so that viewers give the graphic piece a metaphorical meaning.

24 — Ferrer, I. (2002). *El sentido de lo dicho se consume en los silencios.* (Morés, Ed.). Oviedo: Morés Repromorés S.L.

In a conversation with Isidro Ferrer, he told me that the images he uses "are at the service of their own values that are not only iconic but also representative. Therefore, things have meaning because they have a content that grounds them to their shape and message." It is common to see faces in keys, cardboard boxes, stones or pots and pans in his posters and illustrations. The designer makes these everyday objects exceptionally relevant, both within the design itself and for viewers, who can use them to better understand the artwork. "What I want with my posters is for the public to read them: a semantic and meaningful reading," he went on to tell me. Moreover, the textures and ochre colours that he usually applies send messages of tranquillity, relaxation and grounded communication that makes us really feel something.

Although both of the examples included here use human-like characteristics to convey personality, this is not the only way to relate to an audience on a human level. For example, Apple adopted emotional branding by having its devices make gestures that are suggestive of human characteristics—think, for example, of how the standby light of a Mac imitates the breathing pattern of a sleeping person—and the company is now associated with feelings of happiness, enjoyment, playfulness and relaxation. What it is important to appreciate here is that the principles that govern communication between a graphic design piece and a person aren't that different from those which govern communication between people. Just as we would be suspicious of someone whose personality constantly changes, we will lose trust in and begin to question the integrity of a design beset

Isidro Ferrer

Illustrator and designer

What does "emotional design" mean to you?

For me it's tautological. I don't understand something like graphic design as a "creative" activity . . . if it doesn't take emotions into account. Emotion is an ethical and fundamental characteristic of any type of project, whether it is design or not. However, emotion is not entirely positive. It is an agitation of the feelings. That is, when we get emotional, there may be not just pleasurable aspects but also negative and dramatic ones. It seems that emotions are always seen as something positive, but they are actually quite complex and diverse.

I've noticed that a lot of times you use human figures to communicate a message. Do you think that characters of this kind make the design come to life somehow?

I use signs and symbols that are dependent on meaning. What I want with my posters is for the public to read them—a semantic and meaningful reading. I want the reader to unravel the meaning of the image, which is expressly linked with the text that represents it. I want to establish a direct relationship between words and images so that together they can create meaning.

Colours and materials have a great impact on the way in which we assign personality traits to objects. Do you agree with this statement? Do you apply it to your work in any way?

I think materials help with the sensory part, right? We perceive things differently based on the way we sense them. Our touch is linked to our sight and smell. Therefore, our sensory capacity isn't limited to the physical but goes beyond that. The use of materials—when used both graphically and orthographically— communicates a lot of different data according to our own experience.

Do you think that a successful communication benefits from giving personality traits to the graphic work?

Personality is all about style. It isn't something premeditated, but rather a consequence of what I can do with my hands. I mean, I can't do everything I would like to do, right? I used to say that I am the sum of my desires and my own limitations. One thing is the idyllic place I want to be, and another totally different one is the place where my capabilities take me. What we call "style" is not a direct consequence of an intention but rather the consequence of all the limitations one has. And our gestures, hand and calligraphy define what we can do.

Isidro Ferrer: "Frida & Diego", 2008. Poster

frida
&
diego

¡
qué
viva
méxico
!

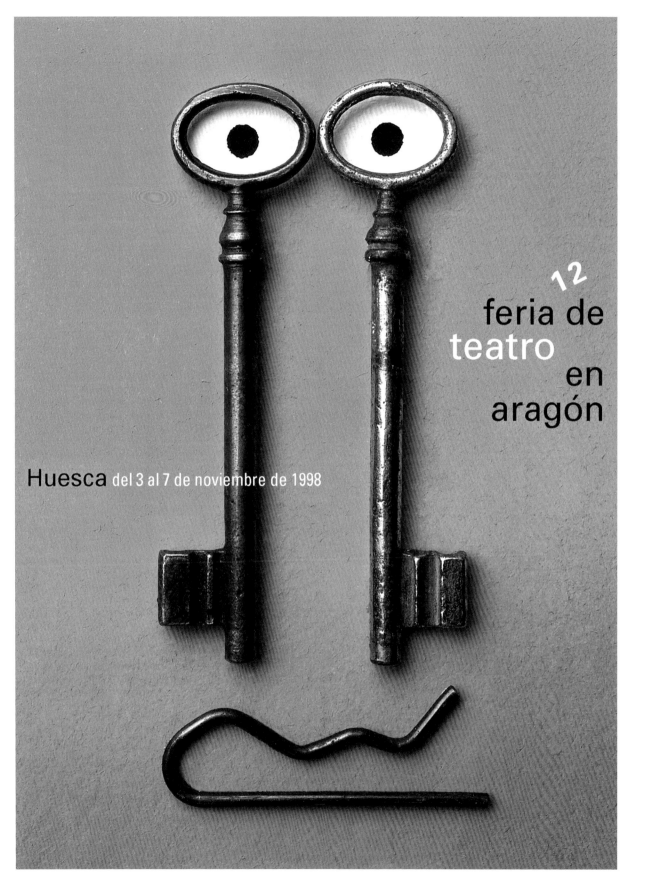

12 feria de teatro en aragón

Huesca del 3 al 7 de noviembre de 1998

by inconsistencies. For this reason, I think it is important for designers to think about how we interact with our friends and to try to apply the same principles in our creations.

Multisensorial

Throughout our lives, it might seem that we use some senses more than others (for example, sight as compared to smell). However, the combination of the five senses is what helps us to better understand and form opinions about the world. Michael Haverkamp, an expert in sound design, describes the theory of a cross-sensory approach in his book *Synesthetic Design*. A multisensory design has a better chance of meeting the public's expectations at all levels by connecting visual, auditory, tactile and olfactory features. These senses allow viewers to better appreciate the identity of the piece and relate with it on a richer emotional level.

It is easier to explore the interplay of multiple sensory features in three-dimensional design pieces. Nevertheless, such an approach could be implemented even when making two-dimensional pieces. Doing so results in a more stimulating experience for viewers, improving the emotional relationship between themselves and the design. To achieve this effect, it is important to align the design environment with the viewer's various senses—that is, the way in which a person interacts with a certain graphic piece should result in a pleasant and harmonious experience that combines all the senses. (Or at least the majority of them: I don't think it would be a good idea to have people licking posters displayed in public!)

There are already special papers on the market that provide olfactory and tactile experiences, allowing an interaction with the audience's sensory channels. For example, there are papers that when rubbed, release a special fragrance when rubbed, react to the body's temperature or even perfectly imitate fabric or skin textures. Texture itself—not necessarily physical texture—is an important communication tool that, unfortunately, is frequently neglected in graphic design. It is the designer's job to find novel techniques that enable the customization and creation of immersive graphic pieces.

In Canada, Somerset—one of the country's top printers—approached the agency Leo Burnett to ask for help in renewing its brand identity and website in order to showcase its capabilities when it comes to completing complex assignments. For Leo Burnett, the challenge was to find a way to

Isidro Ferrer: "12 Feria de Teatro en Aragón," 1998. Poster

‹

show printing—something that is tactile—in a flat and digital environment. The solution came in the shape of a printed website. As Leo Burnett's team put it, "We brought the experience of touching and feeling the page online."[25] The project consisted of a printed sheets of paper that mimicked the size of an actual website and featured interactive details that could work both on and offline. Examples of those details are a GIF made with scanimation, a scratch-off URL bar and tear-off information panels. These techniques were then recorded using stop motion and integrated into the online website. Somerset could have merely taken high-quality photos that illustrated its technical skills. Fortunately, with the help of Leo Burnett, it did much more than that and ended up with a website that delivers a truly tactile experience.

The project consisted in a printed press sheet mimicking the size of an actual website, featuring interactive details that could work both off and online. Examples of those are a GIF made with scanimation, a scratch-off URL bar, and tear-off information panels. These techniques were then recorded using stop motion, and integrated in the online website. Somerset could have contented themselves with taking high-quality photos that illustrated their technical skills. Fortunately, with the help of Leo Burnett, they ended up doing more than that, with a website that recalls a truly tactile experience.

25 — D&AD. (2016). *Case Study: Printed by Somerset*. Retrieved (June 19, 2018) from: https://www.dandad.org/en/d-ad-printed-somerset-case-study-insights/

Tom Inns, director of the AHRC/EPSRC Design for the 21st Century Research Initiative, explains the importance of applying multisensory features in a design by suggesting that "it is through the sense of self that we engage with our emotions, dreams, imagination, and with desires."[26] To take the example of a book (which is a three-dimensional object in itself and is meant to be touched), a designer can increase the pleasure of reading by implementing a multisensorial approach that enhances touch and feel. The more real a book's tangibility is—its weight, texture, surface and heft—the deeper the connection between it and its reader. A book that transcends the norm—that invites the reader to turn it over, fold it up, or even walk inside it—demands more attention and may result in stronger memories.

If the tactile properties of a book are viewed as part of its content and not just as the medium of the message, people will be more eager to explore the book, feel part of it and assimilate all of its existence. Sometimes it is difficult to communicate ideas using only words, and yet stories continue to be told using only text. Couldn't a book

26 — Inns, T. (2007). *Designing for the 21st Century — Interdisciplinary Questions and Insights*. (Tom Inns, Ed.) (1st ed.). Hampshire: Gower Publishing Limited.

⟩

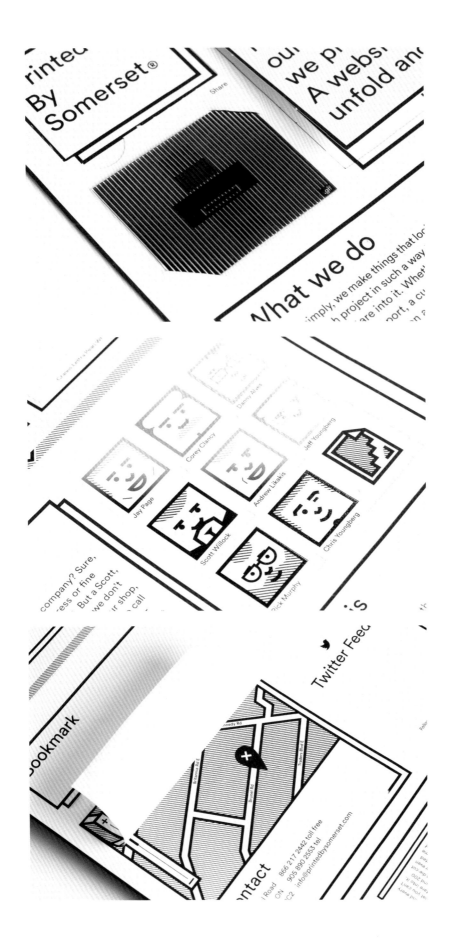

take advantage of its tactile characteristics and stimulate other senses in order to tell better stories? The London-based book publisher Visual Editions believes it is possible to do so. With a commitment to telling stories in a different way, Britt Iversen and Anna Gerber, the firm's cofounders, offer new experiences to their readers and writers, one book at a time.

By using innovative formats, layouts, and technology, Visual Editions makes one-of-a-kind, revolutionary publications that aim to delight the minds and senses of their readers. One example is Jonathan Safran Foer's *Tree of Codes*. To make this book, the author took an old novel and cut out the words to give form to his new story—a technique that can be compared to a sculptor who takes chunks out of a block of marble to create his imagined piece. The result is a tactile book with die-cut words that explores the relationship between its pages and gives shape to a meaningful narrative.

Other books by Visual Editions don't always feature the same degree of tactile engagement, but they certainly *do* explore the relationship between visuals and text, as well as the way in which the reading experience can be enhanced through this relationship. *Composition No.1* is a collection of single pages in a box that can be read in any order, thus breaking the idea of a linear narrative. *Kapow!* invites readers to get lost in the narrative by having them fold and unfold pages and turn the book around to follow the varied orientation of the paragraphs. There are many more examples beyond those mentioned here, and their existence demonstrates how versatile and effective it can be for a designer to play with books and their narratives.

Britt and Anna get their motivation to continue innovating in the publishing sector from the increasingly digitized world that we live in. In an interview in *It's Nice That* magazine, Visual Editions' cofounders explained that they "think that for a book to merit being printed, there's got to be something about that experience that can only live on the page. . . . A sculptural object that has a story, that you can read. That kind of tactile, sensory experience you just can't replicate on the screen."[27]

The publishing duo has since decided to explore interactive digital narratives that follow its ethos of designing what they call "good looking stories." The important thing in their view

27 — Hudson, W. (2010, September). "Visual Editions," in *It's Nice That*. Retrieved from: https://www.itsnicethat.com/articles/3100-visual-editions

is to focus on the story and find the best way to tell it, whether it is through an app, an event or a printed book. However, the multisensory nature of books is, in my opinion, what pleases and surprises the public the most. As a designer, I believe we should strive for these kinds of unexpected and pleasurable experiences that spark real emotions.

Discoverability

Discoverability refers to the ability of something to be found. It could be the date of an event on the poster advertising that event, or it could be the appearance of the name of a product on its label. Finding this information is not very exciting, as the public expects to find it. However, if an unexpected piece of information is found within a given design, it can create a much deeper and more meaningful connection with the viewer. This unexpected piece of information could be the functionality of the design itself—or, to put things more accurately, the extra functionality. For example, what if a book was made not just to be read or a poster was designed not only to communicate a specific message? A viewer will likely experience pleasure in finding that design pieces can be used for other things beyond the expected purposes. For example, imagine a book made from materials that are so soft and fluffy that it could be used as a pillow once you felt tired of reading it, or one that not only provided information to the world's poorest communities about the risks of drinking polluted water but also provided a means to prevent them from doing so.

This last example is not just something that I have imagined. It is the outcome of a collaboration between the creative agency DDB New York, the charitable organization WATERisLIFE and Dr. Theresa Dankovich, a chemist from Carnegie Mellon University. *The Drinkable Book* is a hundred-page volume that provides its reader with clean water for up to four years. The book is made from a special paper invented by Dankovich that works as a high-tech filter that eliminates almost all of the bacteria responsible for waterborne diseases such as cholera, E. coli, and typhoid.

Most readers of this book will have been raised in an environment in which we have access to clean water and are taught in school that the quality of the water that you drink has a very important impact on your health and survival. However, there are still 1.8 billion people in the world who lack access to safe drinking water, and many of them will die from water-borne diseases just because they aren't fully aware of the dangers of drinking polluted water. This stark reality demonstrates the need for the creation and distribution of *The Drinkable Book*. This project not only raises awareness about the importance of proper sanitation and hygiene practices but also provides a way to access clean water. Kristine Bender, president of WATERisLIFE, says that "a book is a treasured possession, and one that stirs emotion and feelings. This is a brilliant and innovative execution of a simple tool to provide life's most basic need—clean water."[28]

Visual Editions: (bottom) "Tree of Codes," 2010. Book design / (top) "Composition No.1," 2011. Book design

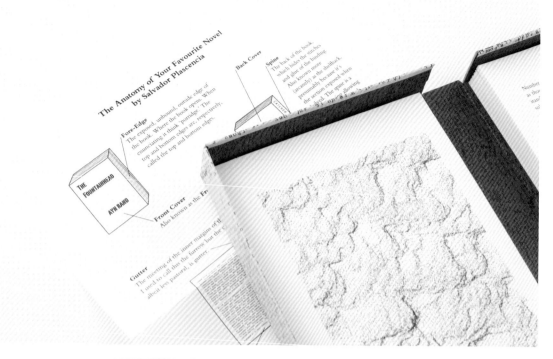

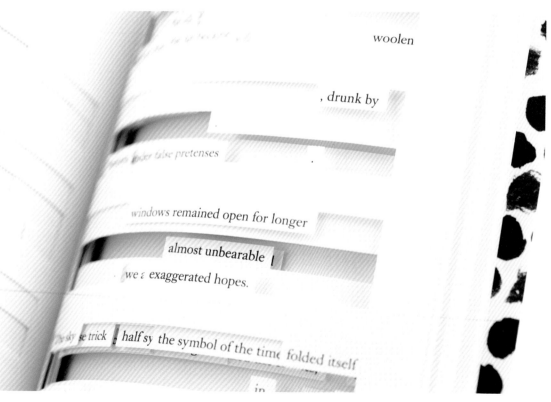

The New York-based typographer Brian Gartside, who collaborates with DDB New York, was the individual who came up with the idea of turninging Dankovich's invention into a guidebook. Education was a cornerstone of the project, which led the designer to divide each page into two sections. The top section provides instructions in English, while the bottom one is written in local languages (for example, Swahili). The book begins as follows: "The water in your village may contain deadly diseases. But each page of this book is a paper water filter that will make it safe to drink." More specific directions then follow. The text is printed using a food-based ink so as not to contaminate the water with other harmful components. A custom-made box for the book is designed to work as a receptacle in which the reader can place one page and pour unclean water through it to produce water that is pure and safe to drink. It was designed as a product that could fit into the normal lives of these populations so that it could be easily adopted and used. In the end, this is not just a book; it is a lifesaver. Wouldn't it be great if more graphic pieces could be beneficial for humankind?

It is possible to come up with ground-breaking ideas by exploring the space "outside the box," reevaluating our assumptions and creating new opportunities with the materials available to us. This is not an easy task, but rewarding the public with a hidden meaning inside an otherwise simple message is something that encourages engagement. In fact, curiosity is one of the basic human needs, and it is what creates our desire to explore what's in front of us and to see if there is something more that we are missing. For example, if you saw pictures of letter stencils—like the ones used before computers were even a thing—displayed around a city, you'd probably ask yourself what they were trying to communicate. This was the imagery used in the first flyer for the Compact Discothéque's evening sessions, hosted by the DJ and designer Nuno Coelho at the Triplex bar in Porto. Contemplating the space-saving way in which letters were arranged on stencils, Coelho thought about how convenient it would be for the letters to be organized according to the information that he wanted to communicate. And so the Compact Discothéque's flyer collection was born.

28 — Kaplan, M. (2014, September 20). "Filtering water by the book," in *Impact*. Retrieved from: http://impactjournalsmday.com/story/filtering-water-by-the-bookby/

Each month between 2003 and 2007, Coelho came up with a different way of advertising the party inspired by the graphic arts and the different means of communication we have (or had) at our disposal. Flyers that looked like traced letters, notebooks, colouring books, fridge magnet, post-its and Morse code were distributed across Porto to advertise these

Nuno Coelho

Communication designer

What does emotional design mean to you?

I think in this field, emotional design isn't just a pragmatic design whose goal is only to communicate a message but rather a design that creates a deeper connection with the public. Taking the specific example of my work for Compact Discothéque; these were informative flyers that also had the goal of captivating and persuading people to go to the party. Because of that, they had to have a distinctive character, something that was different from what we are used to seeing around us. It's likely that what is different attracts more attention to it. However, it wasn't fortuitous; I looked for a special reaction from the public. I think that is the purpose of communication: not only to be informative but also engaging.

How did you come up with the idea for Compact Discothéque's flyers?

Being my own boss at Triplex, I started doing something I wasn't able to do until then: using a different visual universe from what is the norm when the focus is night life and parties by finding unconventional ways to use existing communicational tools. When I refer to this project, I never show the first two or three flyers because they're different from the collection I ended up creating. The final idea came more or less by chance. I was using letter templates for some other project and realized that the alphabet was not in order. Instead of being ABCD, it was AI3CD to save space on the template (the I is also the number 1 and the I and 3 together make the letter B). I recall looking at it and thinking how convenient it would be if my information was already ordered on the template instead of having to move around to choose the right letters.

The idea for the first flyer of the collection was born from this thought. The reaction from my group of friends was really good and a lot of people came to me to comment on the flyer, so I realized I couldn't do anything less on the next one. So I started thinking about other flyer ideas that could make up a collection. The second idea that came to my mind was using tracing letters; from there I started searching for tools and ways of communicating that we used at the time or that were obsolete (such as sign language and Morse code) to create a logical collection of flyers. That is the concept of this project.

How do you innovate and avoid clichés?

I think innovation has a lot to do with a local way of thinking. I see those flyers as metanarratives because people will only understand the joke if they know the object I use as a referent. I think innovation has to do with the logic of thought and not so much with a specific method or tool.

Nuno Coelho: "Compact Discothéque," 2003-7. Flyers

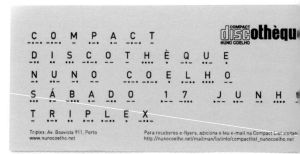

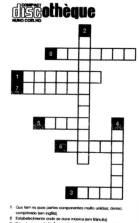

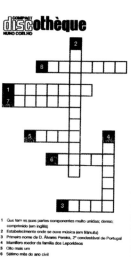

DJ sessions. The designer wanted the information to be "simple, easy to read, direct and, as far as possible, interactive, in the hope of receiving a reaction from the audience."[29] And after he realized that partygoers were eagerly anticipating the next month's flyer, Coelho decided to embed some entertaining and challenging features within the design. He partially hid the information so people had to make an extra effort to figure out what was being communicated. For instance, the advertising for the first anniversary of Compact Discothéque's sessions could only be read by using backlighting, as the asymmetric letters were printed on the front of the paper and the symmetric ones on the back. "The flyers were welcomed by the public, and I felt like they would appreciate a bit of a challenge," Nuno explains.

All of the flyers had the same 7 x 15 cm measurements. Coelho explains that this conformity was a simple way to convey the collection's coherence and help people to see each flyer as being part of a whole set. In fact, Nuno told me with a laugh that some people even sent him emails asking for flyers that they hadn't had the chance to grab, as though they were missing cards from a collection.

29 — *Catálogo Jovens Criadores.* (2003). Lisbon: CPAI.

For me, the way in which Coelho appropriates the banal and things that would likely pass unnoticed to use them in unexpected ways is something very refreshing. "Look at things as if it was the first time," advises the designer. "By doing this, we can sometimes notice what is inherent to our culture, which we probably don't appreciate enough. We can get a lot of innovative material from that, which makes all the difference. This culture is only made by us, the Portuguese public. Some aspects of the flyers will only be understood by someone who lived in the country." No one said that all graphic design must be universal, and in this case, working for a specific audience was the best way to achieve an emotional connection.

One of the key principles of discoverability to keep in mind is that it should be easy for the audience to discover the second meaning just by playing around with the design. If a message is too hidden, people might not ever find it, and so the entire purpose of integrating a second function or piece of information into a design will become pointless.

While it is true that some projects should be clearer than water (see the next principle to understand what I mean), by putting some thought into our designs, we can make them carry a double meaning. This process shouldn't be difficult, as we have been doing it throughout our lives. For example, when we were children, we used our sofa as a fortress or our parents' pots and pans as a noisy drum set. The design could end up being childish and pointless, but it could also be one of our most meaningful projects.

Clarity

The previous principles make it clear that one way to express emotions in graphic design is to enhance the interactive experience offered by a piece. Whereas under the discoverability principle this enhancement is the result of finding unexpected additional information, under the clarity principle emotion is elicited by the clarification of the information that the public expects to find. After all, a design piece usually has the main goal of providing information to its viewers—information that should be easily recognizable and sufficiently understandable so as not to cause confusion. Consider the example of a poster that announces an event. When people look at it, they inherently expect to find the date of the event and what it is about. If this information is disguised or hard to find, it will probably cause frustration for the viewer, making the poster and the work put into it useless.

Usually, the information arrangement chosen by designers is obvious to them. However, it may not be so obvious to the public. A designer should understand what the public knows about the subject and what their expectations and limitations are when learning new things. With these insights, designers can prototype tangible ideas and gather people's input about them, which will most likely lead to an effective graphic communication. It is advisable to make use of layout, information architecture and typography to break data down into small units that won't overwhelm the audience.

This isn't something new. In the 1950s, the pioneers of Swiss graphic design were already using what they called the "complexity of the simple,"[30] which means bringing order to complex information by reducing statements until an objective message is reached. Their rational style demanded there to be a reason and purpose behind all design decisions, and as a result, it is hard to find any unnecessary elements within their pieces.

When one talks about Swiss graphic design, it is almost impossible not to refer to the work of Joseph Müller-Brockmann, a designer from the 1940s and 1950s whose poster design work reflected a neutral, functional and objective style. His commitment to clear, intuitive design was based on the premise that design should be enjoyable for the public. In his words, "Just as

30 — Müller-Brockmann, J. (2007). *Josef Müller-Brockmann: Pioneer of Swiss graphic design.* (L. Müller, Ed.) (4th ed.). Baden: Lars Müller Publishers.

Josef Müller-Brockmann: "5. Frühjahrskonzert der Tonhalle-Gesellschaft," 1953. Poster. Museum of Modern Art (MoMA). Photolithograph 39 x 27 ¾'. Gift of the Kunstgewerbe Museum, Zurich 332.1957

5. Frühjahrskonzert   der Tonhalle-Gesellschaft
Tonhalle Grosser Saal   Dienstag 19. Mai 1953 20.15 Uhr

Leitung   **Erich Schmid**

Violine   **Hansheinz Schneeberger**

Concerto grosso in F-dur   **A. Vivaldi**

Violinkonzert (1951)   **F. Martin**

Sinfonie Nr. 1, in B-dur, op. 38   **R. Schumann**

Vorverkauf   Tonhallekasse Hug & Co. Jecklin Kuoni

Entwurf J. Müller-Brockmann Satz-Druck

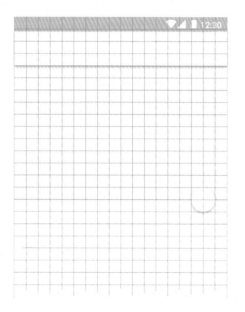

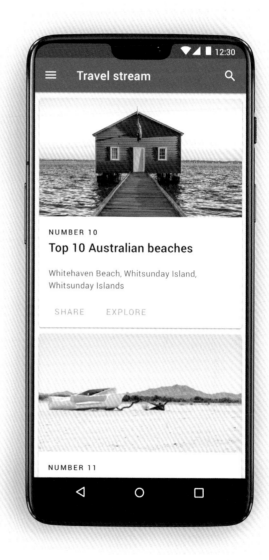

NUMBER 10

Top 10 Australian beaches

Whitehaven Beach, Whitsunday Island,
Whitsunday Islands

SHARE   EXPLORE

NUMBER 11

clear, clean musical forms are pleasant to the listener, and give joy to the knowledgeable in their structure, so clear, pure form and colour should give visual pleasure to the viewer."[31]

His work on the concerts organized by Zurich's local government provides an example of good visual hierarchy and organization that helps focus attention on the important areas of information. The information placement on these posters creates invisible lines, which predetermine, to a certain extent, the spectator's eye movements. It lends musicality and rhythm to the design, in some ways mirroring the classical music compositions being played at the event. Müller-Brockmann published a series of manuals for graphic designers on topics such as grid layouts and information arrangement. In his book *The Graphic Artist and his Design Problems*, the author explains that "a deliberately composed design has a clearer, more neatly arranged and more successful effect than an advertisement put together at random,"[32] and he provides a series of techniques to deliver such clarity. His extensive knowledge of design resources and their effective application, along with his professional ethic and sense of social and cultural responsibility, earned him a high degree of respect from the design community that endures even today.

Sixty years have passed since Müller-Brockmann's book was first published, and during that time graphic design challenges have changed and evolved. In today's world, people get information not only from printed materials but also from digital screens. However, despite the fact that the design canvas has changed, the same guidelines for clarity and organization of information still apply.

Nowadays, designers feel the need to create new mechanisms and resources to guide the audience to the correct understanding of the message, especially because we live in a time when we are easily distracted by the diversity of stimuli competing to capture our attention. Once again, it is important to divide information into manageable blocks, make use of grid systems, and provide users with a sense of orientation to make it easier for them to know where they are, where they can go, and where they've been. After all, regardless of the age, graphic design is seen as a tool for effective and useful communication.

With this understanding in mind, Google developed a design system called Material Design in 2014. The goal was to help design teams to craft the best digital experiences by creating solutions based on grid layouts, responsive animations and transitions, and meaningful *space* indicators.

31 — *Ibid.*

32 — Müller-Brockmann, J. (2003). *The Graphic Artist and his Design Problems*. Zürich: Verlag Niggli AG.

According to Google's designers, this system was created "as a metaphor to rationalize design and implementation, establishing a shared language to help teams unite style, branding, interaction, and motion under a cohesive set of principles. We believe a better design process yields better products, which is why we're expanding Material to be a system that supports the principles of good design and strengthens communication and productivity with new tools and inspiration."[33]

Once again, aesthetic notions were also considered. The choice of a balanced colour palette, flat compositions, simple icons and an intelligent use of depth and shadows conveys a sensible and trustworthy personality to products that use the Material Design system.

33 — Jitkoff, N. (2016). "Design Is Never Done." Retrieved (August 26, 2017) from: https://design.google/library/design-never-done/

I would like to highlight a 1995 conversation between Paul Rand—one of the most famous designers of all time—and the author and art theorist Rudolf Arnheim, who said, "Anything that you want to say clearly and to the point has to have coherence, symmetry, and simplicity."[34] I also believe it is important to mention that simplicity is not easy to achieve, and it shouldn't be confused with boring or uninteresting characteristics. A clear and clean design can bequeath elegance and beauty to a piece, which will in turn draw the audience closer to it. Being aware of this fact can help to put both the rational and creative sides of the brain to work in service of communication.

34 — Arnheim, R. (1997). "Paul Rand and Rudolf Arnheim: Dialogue," in K. Kleinman & L. Van Duzer (Eds.), *Revealing Vision* (pp. 75–87). Michigan: University of Michigan Press.

Candy Chang: "Before I Die," 2011–7. Art project

〉

Before I
Before I die I want to
see The Kinks play again!
Before I die I want to
Before I die I want to
visit my Greek homeland.
Before I die I want to
SEE A TON OF TREES!
Before I die I want to
Before I die I want to
see my 2 sons graduate college
Before I die I want to
Meet My grandchildren!
Before I die I want to
Before I die I want to
Before I die I want to
Before I die I want to
Before I die I want to
Before I die I want to
Before I die I want to
Be heard!
Become Batman!
Stop WAR
Improve my handwriting
KNOW GOD
TAKE A FREE PEDICAB
CELEBRATE 50TH WEDDING ANNIVERSARY
GET PUBLISHED & TRAVEL THROUGH CHINA
GO TO SPAIN
Travel aimlessly
BE A MOTHER
RIDE A WAVE WITH MY DAUGHTER
HAVE A SCHOOL IN SPR!
HANG GLIDE
BUILD A TRUE REGENERATIVE PROJECT
GET PUBLISHED
MEET MY GRANDCHILDREN
OWN A DOG + NESPRESSO COFFEE MACHINE
Remind her why she loves me everyday
Fix us Homeless
Speak Spanish
YES PROP 37 PASSES!
STOP Animal Cruelty
Make a diff. in Mexico
GIVE A TED TALK
FINALIZE MY DIVORCE!
aprender muchos idiomas
Take lots of naps.
EAT MY HONEY
Create
SLEEP WITH JAVIER BARDEM!
RETIRE
Forgive
PERFECT MY PAVEMENT
Travel
Become
Miss America

go to every continent   WIN THE LOTTERY!   REGENE

lie...

I hu...ed

Have a LIVE INSPIRE OTHERS TO DO!

MARRY

BE FORGIVEN

PLANT 1000,00 TREES

Be an astronomer

Follow me

Retire w/ cheryl! ? Konad

IMPEACH OBAMA ✓

Plant a seed of change in every child's mind.

I want to fall in love and start a family after college   MarryRodrigo ♥

enjoy my life

solve climate change!

Grab a

SPACE
ldren's children!
wn house

AY   OFF UNDERGRAD   GRAD SCHOOL   A mom   quiero estar siempre contigo, Kike   sing FREELY   reward wood.   Be content/no happy!   For HER

Inspire, help, l

Before I die I want to _____.

See Leed

HAVE MY TED TALK FOR GREEN SCHOOLS

Before I die I

HOME   BUFFALO WINS A CUP
ME
REVOLUTION
for the Greater

Have an elephant @ Home   START A COFFEE SHOP!   PJ!!
MEET MY KIDS-KIDS   HAVE A BABY ✓
Build my own Home!   MAKE A REAL DIFFERENCE ✓

Live to be 10

Before I die I want to _____.   **Before I die I**

DREAMS
dreams!

MAKE A DIFFERENCE & WATCH IT GROW
learn how to swim   you will live again!!!
go on a spontaneous trip   revive a ghost town ✓

PROVE IM
SOMET
Travel the w

Before I die I want to _____.   **Before I die I**

UT MY LIFE
WIFE
difference
eco BOOK!
N FRANCISCO
LEAVING A GREENER WORLD
REAL LOVE AND
REVER! Be totally content

BECOME GOBERNOR   MAKE A DIFFERENCE
OWN A DOG   Make positive difference!
Be deliriously happy!   go to Japan   I go to Paris.   make someone's life better   Run a Marathon
Be Happy + HEALTHY

Make a diff
ACHIEVE IMMO
FIND PEACE WITH
SEE MY DREA
do a triathlo

Before I die I want to _____.   **Before I die I**

WIN THE SOLAR DECATHLON   Make love to GIADA   LET GO & ENJOY!
2013 - GO Team ASU/NM   MAKE A GREAT MOVIE   WITNESS OUR TRANSITION TO RENEWABLE ENERGY

Before I die I want to _____.   **Before I die I**

married (legally)   Start my own Business   BE A MOTHER   QUIT WORRYING ABOUT MONEY!
TO THE FULLEST   HAVE NO REGRETS!   SEE HALEY'S COMET

MARRY THE
SEE MY CHILDREN

Before I die I want to _____.   **Before I die I**

n this wall
lk!!   truly   help someone
ngry?   TRUELY LOVE SOMEONE

change human behavior   Stop the IMF $ WTO.
MARRY AGAIN WITH

Heliski!

Beat Brea Can

To see the world a better place for every one   Pet a Wombat   I will become a FATHER!   TA   TRUST AGAIN

BE
WIN WHOLE

Write   DIVE IN CUBA WITH JGB!

TURN 5 NIECES AND NEPHEWS INTO 5 GLOBAL CITIZENS!

SHOOT A MOOSE   a figi art book   AND DIRECT A(N US SS) PERFORMANCE

DON'T DIE

KEL BACK
ONCERT!   NO, you don't...   △ the World   ♥ Celebrate a million more Birthdays!   WIN!

I want help in all wome

People tend to connect more deeply with information based on a clear narrative. Although some narratives are local anecdotes, there are common universal human traits that make a story relatable across different countries and cultures.

Narrative

Candy Chang: "Before I Die," 2011–7. Art project

"The quality of the story is a second-rate concern so long as we empathize with the person it is about and care for the one telling it." —FRANK CHIMERO

〈

Universal concerns

There are approximately 7.5 billion people in the world. Each and every single one of us has different hopes, fears, dreams and feelings that are the result of the community we live in, our cultural background and our individual personalities. For this reason, it is very difficult to design something that will speak to everyone. What is attractive to some people is invariably not attractive to others, just as what causes excitement and motivation for some may cause boredom for others.

However, there are things that we could say are universally understood—or, in other words, universally felt. Emotions like fear, anger, sadness, joy, love and happiness are felt equally across cultures and personality types. Apart from some rare and idiosyncratic cases, we are all afraid of dying, and we all dream of being loved and being among people who complete us and make us happy.

Let's consider movies as an example here. The reason why some films enjoy such huge success worldwide relates to the fact that they touch upon some of these universal concerns—love, fear, death or self-esteem. Everyone in the audience, whether they are from the North, the South, the East, or the West, will somehow relate to those scenes and share the same types of emotions. To take this example a little further, it could be argued that although romantic comedies aren't the most intellectual movies, and nor do they add any relevant information to our lives, they engage many people, mostly because the actors' romantic experiences and failures echo audiences' own stories.

Taking these insights to the field of graphic design, the New Yorker artist TRUE applied the universal need for happiness to another worldwide activity: commuting. In all public transportation systems, there is a range of official signs that tell commuters what they should and should not do. In order to lift up the spirits of the community, TRUE covered some of New York's subway signs with more philosophical and optimistic ones, calling the project "Life Instructions." These signs looked exactly like the real ones and blended in perfectly with the subway environment; only the most attentive passengers managed to notice them.

These caring and light-hearted signs "instructed" travellers not to hold grudges, not to despair, to keep their hopes up and to strive for happiness. Although this project was limited to New York subway trains from 1994 to 2014, it could easily be replicated in trains on the other side of the world to evoke the same types of emotions.

TRUE: "Life Instructions," 1994–2014. Public instalation

Do not hold doors

Please

Air Conditioned Car
Please close windows

Riding Between cars prohibited

Keep doors closed

Riding with despair prohibited

Keep hopes up

Please

Karma Conditioned Car
Please watch what you do

 Do not hold grudges

Life Instructions

Have fun

Do not hurt people

Do not accept defeat

Strive to be happy

Evacuation Instructions

Listen for instructions from crew

Do not pull emergency brake

Remain inside train. Subway tracks are dangerous

Exit only when directed

Sparking feelings of happiness is an almost infallible technique that designers can use to get closer to an audience and relate to their personal lives. On the other side of the spectrum, there is sadness. Designs that evoke sadness—by displaying topics such as loss or death, for example—are often discouraged. Everyone feels uncomfortable when talking or hearing about such topics, as they remind us of the ephemeral nature of our lives. As sad as death can be, the strong emotions that come out of this event make us reflect on what is most important to us and on what makes our life meaningful. According to some philosophers, contemplating death helps us to restore perspective and clarity in our lives.[35]

35 — Chang, C. (2013). *Before I Die* (1st ed.). New York: St. Martin's Griffin.

To help citizens bear this difficult burden, Candy Chang's art project *Before I Die* transformed an abandoned house in New Orleans into a giant mural that asked passersby life's ultimate question: What do you want to do before you die? The front façade of the house was covered in charcoal paint and later sprayed with the words "Before I die I want to _____." The combination between the black charcoal and the white letters only intensified the content. In Paul Rand's essay "Black in the Visual Arts," he suggests that these colours "are the raw unaltered colours of the struggle between life and death."[36]

36 — Rand, P. (1968). *A Designer Art*. London: Yale University Press.

The fill-in-the-blanks approach was extremely successful in getting people to share their hopes, fears, dreams and aspirations in a public space, with responses ranging from the humorous to the painful. Despite the artist's concern that people might not engage with the work, the project was embraced. The entire wall was completely filled time and time again; it started conversations between neighbours and transformed a neglected space into a constructive one.

Death and all of the emotions surrounding it aren't just felt by New Orleans's citizens; they are universal. This project resulted in the creation of a toolkit and website—developed by Candy Chang and the activist group Civic Center—that helped individuals around the world to develop a "before I die" wall in their community. Now, more than thirty countries have joined the project, allowing their citizens to share their unique life ambitions. According to Chang, the project's universal appeal comes from "knowing you're not alone; it's about understanding our neighbours in new and enlightening ways; it's about making space for reflection and contemplation, and remembering what really matters most to us as we grow and change."[37]

37 — Chang, C. (2012). "Before I die I want to…" in TED talks. Retrieved from: https://www.ted.com/talks/candy_chang_before_i_die_i_want_to?language=en

TRUE: "Life Instructions," 1994–2014. Public instalation

In conclusion, graphic design pieces that reflect on basic universal concerns are more likely to elicit equally common emotions and to engage with a larger audience. In times when war, greed, anger and inequality still play a major role in the world's societies, we, as designers, could try to appeal to basic human concerns by making use of our creativity to mitigate such negative emotions. Graphic design has enough power to successfully communicate messages that the world needs, such as information pertaining to health, conflict resolution, human rights and democracy.

Storytelling

There is a quote from the writer Janet Litherland that in my opinion perfectly conveys why graphic design should tell stories: "Stories have power. They delight, enchant, touch, recall, inspire, motivate, challenge. They imprint a picture on our minds. Want to make a point or raise an issue? Tell a story."[38] As a motor of numerous emotional experiences, stories are engaging and powerful tools that help us relate to various messages. When we communicate with others, we often do so through dialogues and stories. If we look at our personal experiences, we also find that we generally prefer to read a story rather than a list of dreary data and will usually better process and retain information using the former method rather than the latter one. If the purpose of graphic design is to establish a conversation with an audience—in which the audience provides feedback on the design piece—then its method of communication should follow the same logic.

In brand design, telling a story is a great way to create and strengthen emotional connections between the design itself and its audience. People will better understand and more easily internalize the soul of a brand (its mission, vision and values) when it is communicated as a story. Moreover, the better a person feels they know a brand, the easier it will be to trust it and to decide to make it a part of their life.

38 — Litherland, J. (2011). "The Power of Storytelling." Retrieved (May 2, 2015) from: http://www.dragonfly-effect.com/blog/the-power-of-storytelling/

When designing to communicate information, it is essential to find a good narrative behind the information. Discovering interesting facts about the data or message that are worth sharing will help shape the design and engage the viewer. Designers' careful eye for detail has the potential to find the hero of the story that will guide the design approach and make the piece extraordinary to look at. In the same way that readers expect to

Tom Haugomat and DDB Paris: "Volkswagen illustrated campaign," 2015. Advertising campaign

〉

If they lie to their kids, what will they tell you when they sell you their car ?

Used cars you can trust.
Guaranteed.

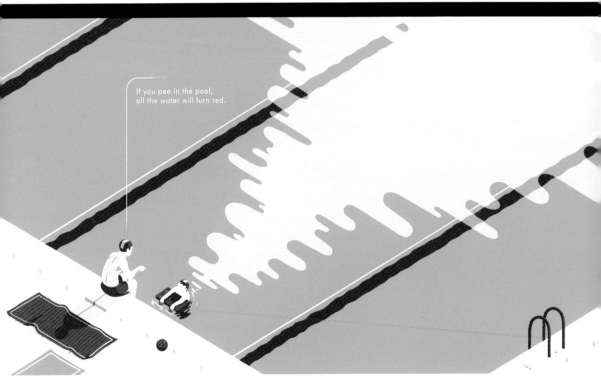

If they lie to their kids, what will they tell you when they sell you their car ?

Used cars you can trust.
Guaranteed.

If they lie to their kids, what will they tell you when they sell you their car ?

If they lie to their kids, what will they tell you when they sell you their car ?

see a moral at the end of a story; viewers expect to find a purpose within a design.

A great example of using narrative to relate to the audience can be seen in a campaign developed by DDB for Volkswagen's used-car programme, "Das WeltAuto." The illustration-based posters, created by the French artist Tom Haugomat, depict a variety of scenarios where parents tell their children white lies. The use of blue and red visuals as well as negative space is combined with classic parenting lines. These are followed by the tagline "If they lie to their kids, what will they tell you when they sell you their car?"

We've all told lies to protect people whom we care about, which makes this whimsical metaphor a gentle but compelling way to prevent Volkswagen customers from visiting untrustworthy used-car salesmen and to promote use of the company's official services instead. Notice that Volkswagen itself and the purpose of the campaign are only mentioned at the end. What the viewer sees first is a relatable story that they can empathize with.

Translating information into stories is not an easy job. Only designers who possess analytical judgement and carefully study the information over and over again come close to getting the essence of a message and to explaining it with meaningful visuals. The story told must have some relevance to the message to be delivered. Otherwise, it won't have the desired outcome. Commonplace metaphors and unimaginative images will tear the entire design apart and provide the viewer with little reason to pay attention to it. Communicating a message through a visual narrative can create a strong impact, but doing so successfully requires a full understanding of the underlying motivations behind and the desired impact of the project.

Matt Dorfman is the art director of the *New York Times Book Review*, a freelance designer and an illustrator for publishers and cultural institutions, and he has created pieces that beautifully leverage visual narratives. His book cover illustrations cleverly combine collage—a great resource for linking seemingly unrelated ideas into a single whole—with drawing, creative typography and smart graphic resources within the book's narrative, making people judge the work by its cover.

According to Dorfman, visual storytelling is not easy. He says of his process: "I read whatever I'm asked to respond to by looking for the idea in the text or in the brief that cajoles the most significant emotional response out of me. Then I think really really hard about what that response looks like. This forces me to think about style as a narrative agent and less about whatever my look is. It's time consuming and rife with blind alleys but it keeps things surprising."[39] Only in this way can he continue to come up

Tom Haugomat and DDB Paris: "Volkswagen illustrated campaign," 2015. Advertising campaign with interesting, clever and original content every time he takes on a new project.

By abandoning the literal approach and by striving for more imaginative, entertaining and engaging ways of presenting information, you can please not only your audience but also yourself as a designer. The good thing is that.

39 — Newman, R. (2016). "Art Director / Illustrator Profile - Matt Dorfman: My first big break was a rejection." Retrieved (August 27, 2017) from: https://www.ai-ap.com/publications/article/16759/art-director-illustrator-profile-matt-dorfman.html

And you can apply this principle to all kind of projects. It is true that some messages are easier than others to translate, but even a corporate organization's yearly report can be designed to be more understandable, interesting and memorable. Just think about how you make friends and engage with other people. By applying the same rules of interaction to graphic design, communication will look more natural and will in turn be more rewarding and fulfilling for your audience.

Matt Dorfman: (left) *The Psychopath Test*, 2012. Book cover / (right) *The Professor in the Cage*, 2015. Book cover

THE

PSYCHOPATH
TEST

A
JOURNEY
THROUGH
THE
MADNESS
INDUSTRY

JON RONSON

BESTSELLING AUTHOR OF *THEM* AND
THE MEN WHO STARE AT GOATS

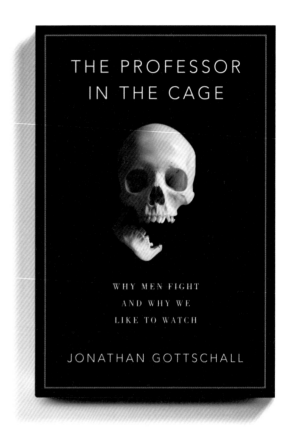

THE PROFESSOR
IN THE CAGE

WHY MEN FIGHT
AND WHY WE
LIKE TO WATCH

JONATHAN GOTTSCHALL

Book Review

The New York Times
OCTOBER 27, 2013 $2

MATT DORFMAN

The Elusive President

By Jill Abramson

AS THE 50TH ANNIVERSARY of his assassination nears, John F. Kennedy remains all but impossible to pin down. One reason is that his martyrdom — for a generation of Americans still the most traumatic public event of their lives, 9/11 notwithstanding — has obscured much about the man and his accomplishments.

Was Kennedy a great president, as many continue to think? Or was he a reckless and charming lightweight or, worse still, the first of our celebrities-in-chief? To what extent do his numerous personal failings, barely reported during his lifetime but amply documented since, overshadow or undermine his policy achievements? And what of those achievements — in civil rights and poverty, to name two issues his administration embraced. Weren't the breakthroughs actually the doing of his successor, Lyndon B. Johnson?

Even the basic facts of Kennedy's death are still subject to heated argument. The historical consensus seems to have settled on Lee Harvey Oswald as the lone assassin, but conspiracy speculation abounds — involving Johnson, the C.I.A., the mob, Fidel Castro or a baroque combination of all of them. Many of the theories have been circulating for decades and have now found new life on the Internet, in Web sites febrile with unfiltered and at times unhinged musings.

Of course the Kennedy fixation is hardly limited to the digital world. An estimated 40,000 books about him have been published since his death, and this anniversary year has loosed another vast outpouring. Yet to explore the enormous literature is to be struck not by what's there but by what's missing. Readers can choose from many books but surprisingly few good ones, and not one really outstanding one.

It is a curious state of affairs, and some of the nation's leading historians wonder about it. "There is such fascination in the country about the anniversary, but there is no great book about Kennedy," Robert Caro lamented when I spoke to him not long ago. The situation is all the

CONTINUED ON PAGE 22

Emotional design does not necessarily imply positive emotions. Combining both positive and negative feelings may yield unique and interesting pieces that provoke viewers and capture their attention. This effect can be achieved by playing to the primal part of the human brain and breaking the rules of propriety and decency, or by using strong and impactful imagery that creates controversial and realistic communication.

Paradoxical emotions

Matt Dorfman: "The Elusive President," 2013. Newspaper cover

"To push the boundaries, you need to know where the edges are." —MARK BOULTON

Raw

"Can I eat it? Can I have sex with it? Will it kill me?" We unconsciously ask one or more of these three questions every time we encounter a new subject, whether it is alive—a person or an animal—or is an inanimate item such as food. These three little questions have helped human beings to evolve and get to the point we are at now. They made us stay away from possible threats and avoid things that could put our survival at risk. Along with these questions, humans also developed the feeling of disgust: the feeling we physically exteriorize to remind ourselves and others that something isn't right and that we probably shouldn't interact with it. Disgust works as a powerful emotional warning sign, providing the physical sensation we get when we are faced with things like rotten food, excrement or signs of ill health such as wounds or rashes. So why do we sometimes feel attracted to these same elements? Why do we exhibit kinky behaviours such as being drawn to gory movies, poop jokes or visceral images? Why do humans want to somehow go against the survival rules set by Mother Nature? Are we that perverse?

There is a scientific and psychological answer to these urges: "It's similar to why people go on roller coasters. You feel fear, even though you know you're safe," says Alexander J. Skolnick, assistant psychology professor at Saint Joseph's University. "You get a big arousal value out of them."[40] The point is to feel the rush of adrenaline and arousal caused by repulsive elements, but to do so within a safe environment where the probability of actually interacting with them is practically nonexistent.

Disgust is a potent emotion, and as such using it in graphic design can be very effective. One may assume that the use of imagery that is likely to cause distaste for viewers will, in turn, capture their attention and more effectively convey information. While this may be true, it is also the case that designers are driven by ethical standards. These standards mean that the deliberate use of such imagery—with the sole purpose of appealing to the audience's subconscious survival instinct—is rarely appropriate, and it may even be offensive.

40 — Menza, K., & J. Skolnick, A. (2015, September). "There's a Reason Why We Like to Click on Gross Stuff on the Internet. Shape." Retrieved from: http://www.shape.com/lifestyle/mind-and-body/theres-reason-why-we-click-gross-stuff-internet

Subtly drawing on such emotions, the Spanish graphic designer and typographer Alex Trochut creates typographic compositions that intimate bodily fluids and the like. Causing disgust is not the intention of the artist—or at least not his prime concern—but the organic and gooey strokes of

Alex Trochut: "Time Out London: Brunch," 2015. Magazine cover

>

Time Out
London

The best meal
of the day
covered

MAY 19-25 2015 No.2329
TIMEOUT.COM/LONDON

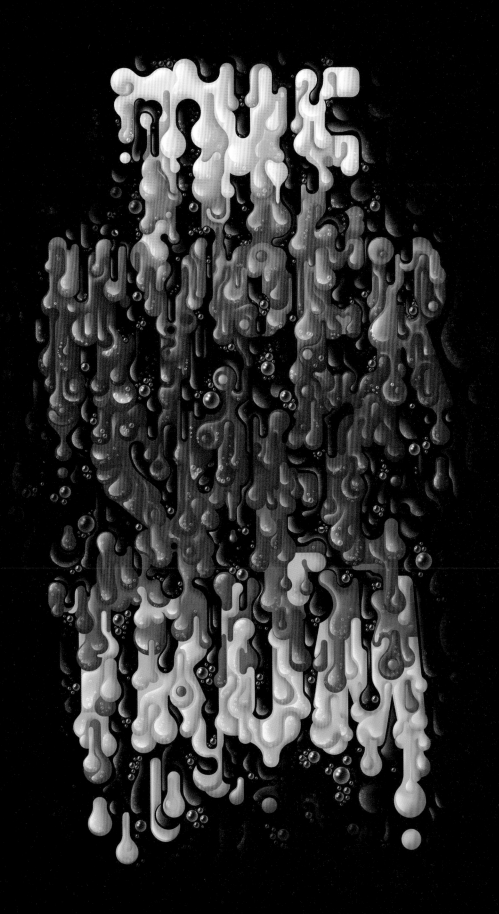

the typography do have a peculiar and visceral charm. Trochut's success is a clear example of the possibility of creating dazzling graphics with what could otherwise be seen as repulsive techniques. Dani Navarro, cofounder of the design studio Forma, describes this branch of Trochut's work as "only just-readable, beautiful, organic, dimensional, colourful, original, and still today: incredible."[41]

In my opinion, Alex Trochut manages to incorporate realistic viscosity only to the point where it is not considered disgusting. In fact, when I come across a piece of Trochut's lettering work, I cannot look away. The movement, fluidity and experimental features of his designs tickle the most visceral part of my brain and entice me into the visual abundance that they create without my finding them repellent.

Strong visceral graphics can be effectively applied when they are accompanied by a concept that elicits positive emotions from the viewer. In fact, as Peter Desmet states in his book *Designing Emotions* (2002), "It would be naïve to assume that to serve the well-being of humans, one should design products that elicit only pleasant emotions. It may be much more interesting to design products that elicit 'paradoxical emotions,' that is positive and negative emotions simultaneously."[42]

"Raw design," as I prefer to call it—rather than "disgusting design"—has to be founded on a strong concept that validates and explains the use of repulsive imagery. When we take our first look at the Hans Brinker Hostel campaigns, we may feel a certain sense of revulsion and nausea or shivers going down our spine, and our face might even contract in disgust. However, this discomfort is rapidly replaced by laughter and amusement as we appreciate the nonsense of it all. What hotel would have thought of advertising itself not for its best qualities but for the absolute worst?

Erik Kessels, cofounder of KesselsKramer, the Amsterdam-based studio behind Brinker's campaign, was quite candid about it: "It was a terrible hotel! It smelled bad, looked horrible. . . . Maybe honesty is the only luxury it had, the only possibility to work with."[43] Both the studio and client soon realised that this approach was having huge success among backpackers and students, as it appealed to their sense of humour. They had found the perfect audience for the brutal irony and nasty honesty of the campaign. In addition, the hostel had also found itself in a marketing niche, as no other accommodation in the world would present "pubic hairball, dead mice, toenail clippings kept in a glass jar" as its decorations.

41 — Dani Navarro. (2011). *Alex Trochut. More is More.* Barcelona: Index Book.

42 — Desmet, P. *Op. cit.*.

43 — Kessels, E. (2016). Lecture Erik Kessels. Barcelona: Elisava. Retrieved from: https://youtu.be/R_C-CdLU-w8w

Erik Kessels

Graphic designer, co-founder of KesselsKramer

Let's have a look at the tools you use to make a change. With regards to your Hans Brinker hostel campaign, you said that "the only luxury of the hotel was honesty." Can honesty really be a tool for advertising? Can you build a strong brand on being honest?

Yes, but it doesn't work for everybody. Being honest, human, ironic or humorous—those are all ways to be more open, explicit and eccentric and to connect with the audience. Those are really good tools to use. Irony is a very good tool because advertising normally doesn't laugh on its own account, so it is good for a company to be a bit ironic about itself. Being honest or very realistic also works, because a lot of advertising is not realistic; it is almost lying a little bit.

Could you give me an example?

When we did a campaign for Ben, they had low prices and said they wanted to be for everyone. So we told them, OK, if that is what you want to do, then you should do exactly that. That means that you also show the minorities in the country, that you show migrants in your ads, that you show a multicultural society and include old people, because that is everybody then. Other phone brands visualize a target group that is almost nonexistent: the family that is always perfect and happy and laughing.

Isn't it the case that people actually like to be lied to and shown all these polished products and smiling faces? And so couldn't something like honesty actually scare them off?

You could think that, but the generation that is living now was born and raised with advertising. They recognize and distinguish all the techniques and know all the aspects of it. It is a bit stupid to think this would work over and over and over again for everybody. To stand still is not really the way forward.

You also concentrate on imperfection, failure and mistakes. But what agencies do for clients usually needs to lead in the direction of perfection. How does that work?

It has a lot to do with the fact that we live in an age when everything is perfect. The telephones that we use and the cameras on them are so perfect that we almost need applications to fuck them up again. To make the pictures a little bit worse. We have navigation systems so we always end up at the right spot. It is the same with the tools for creatives: all the computers are perfect. But perfection is not really a good start for creatives. That is not where you start. You start with chaos and confusion and disruption, because otherwise you never find something else. You need to make a mistake to innovate and to go on.

Extracted from Garaj, P. (2017). *Erik Kessels. Backstage Talks – Dialogues on Design and Business*, 70–77.

KesselsKramer: "Hans Brinker Budget Hotel," 1996–. Campaign

IMPROVE YOUR IMMUNE SYSTEM

THE HANS BRINKER BUDGET HOTEL AMSTERDAM   +31 20 622 0687

Check in

HANS BRINKER BUDGET HOTEL
AMSTERDAM 00 31 20 6220687

Check out

HANS BRINKER BUDGET HOTEL
AMSTERDAM 00 3

HANS BRINKER BUDGET HOTEL. IT CAN'T GET ANY WORSE.

BUT WE'LL DO OUR BEST.
AMSTERDAM +31 20 6220687

Among Brinker's various unseemly campaigns, I would like to highlight the ones that both repulse and fascinate me the most. The *Shit* campaign was the first one undertaken for the hostel by KesselsKramer, and it established the narrative template for future campaigns for the hostel and also the limits that they would be kept within. Little flags with the words "Now more of this at our main entrance" along with Hans Brinker's address were placed at every pile of dog faeces found around Amsterdam's train station. The campaign was aimed at newcomers who would arrive at the city by train, and it was then picked up by media networks across the globe, including CNN, MTV and ABC.

What followed was a series of posters and TV spots advertising Brinker's other (anti) amenities. In the *Check-In/Check-Out* campaign, the young and fresh looking guests who check into the hostel look in much worse shape when they check out. The *Improve Your Immune System* campaign claimed that high levels of bacteria and dirt were intentionally left all over the hostel's installations so that guests' lymph nodes could benefit from the uncleanliness. This positive take on grime led to a before-and-after campaign: *It can't Get Any Worse*, which focused on how serious problems with the hostel were fixed using Brinker's standard methods. In the end, it was impossible not to take notice of this small Amsterdam hostel, which was the purpose behind the campaigns. As a collection of texts about the hostel published by KesselsKramer notes, "Hate. Adoration. Disgust. The Brinker elicits anything except indifference. Writings about the hostel: wherever they're from and whatever their background, these authors are united by their capacity to get very emotional about the little hotel with the big attitude problem."[44]

44 — KesselsKramer. (2009). *The Worst Hotel in the World: The Hans Brinker Budget Hotel Amsterdam (First)*. United Kingdom: Booth-Clibborn Editions.

The ideas that I talked about in this chapter have been used by artists for a long time. Marcel Duchamp, Damien Hirst and Jeff Koons, for example, create controversial and crude art pieces that elicit mixed feelings of both repulsiveness and attraction. Where graphic design is concerned, one might ask if this kind of communication is acceptable. We could say it all depends on the product that is being advertised and on whether or not one is being faithful to its core identity. There's no harm in teasing the audience a little bit by blurring the boundaries between love and hate and political correctness, as long as you have a strong concept that supports doing so.

Scandal

I'd like you to stop and take a look at the advertising that you see around you, whether it's on the street, in magazines or on your Instagram feed. How many ads do you see that don't promise eternal youth, instant fame or an easier life? Very few, right? Ads don't show the difficulties that we may face in our lives simply because—or so advertisers believe—reminding us of life's problems would cause distress for viewers and make them look away. Yet the reason why many advertising campaigns lack strength, impact and common sense is because they fail to acknowledge that reality is sometimes imperfect, and so they come across as making unrealistic promises.

While this may be true, it is also true that negative emotions tend to have a greater influence on behaviour change.[45] When we look at something dramatic or unpleasant, our brain demands more attention and deals with that information differently. We become aroused by strong and negative imagery; it makes us realize that something is wrong. Graphic design and advertising shouldn't leave negative emotions aside completely, as they can motivate the public to reflect, take a position and even act on a certain subject.

45 — van Gorp, T., & Adams, E. *Op. cit.*

Still, the use of such images should be considered. Scandalous imagery shouldn't be used lightly. As designers, we have a responsibility to inform and educate our audience. We shouldn't let this obligation go to waste by creating something that wasn't really thought through just to make a point. Instead, scandalous images can be used to raise critical, cultural, social or political awareness.

Let's take a look at Benetton's advertising campaigns from 1982 to 2000, led by the Italian photographer Oliviero Toscani. Both the brand and the photographer believed that this global retailer company had a moral duty to its customers. The ads were used as a tool for social criticism with the aim to make people think. Addressing society's taboos of the time (AIDS, the death penalty and racism, for example), they were sometimes shocking and never less than controversial.

Toscani believed that, as with any other means of communication, brand advertising should also document and draw attention to what is happening in the world. For him, a brand and a newspaper were exactly the same thing: both had the responsibility to report on current events. That is why the ads in the Benetton campaigns have nothing more than a logo to connect them directly to the brand. There was no need for further information, as the photographs were strong and self-explanatory, and people already knew

Oliviero Toscani: "Hearts," 1996. Campaign

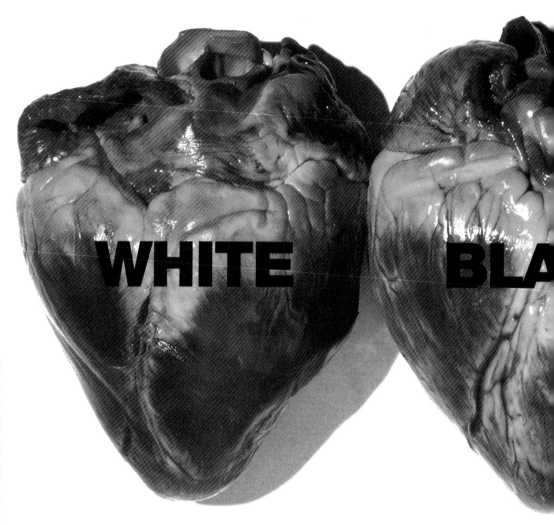

WHITE **BLA**

K YELLOW

UNITED COLORS
OF BENETTON.

what products Benetton offered. Instead, the photographer took advantage of the advertising space and transformed it into "an offer to the public," where he "explored all the domains of creativity and the imaginary, of documentary and of reportage, of irony and provocation; to report on all issues, to serve the great humanitarian causes, to make artists known, to popularize the great discoveries, to educate the public, to be useful and avant-garde."[46] These images had a much stronger emotional impact than those one would find in any standard advertising campaign.

Contrary to what many advertising specialists said at the time, this approach didn't undermine the brand's market position. In fact, various studies on brand recognition conducted in 1994 placed United Colors of Benetton in the top five, beating luxury brands like Chanel. This achievement was undoubtedly the result of Toscani's provocative photography, which represented an approach that had never been seen before in the advertising world. According to the Sarajevo-based creative agency TRIO, "Toscani exposes in his photographs the horror of the world; immortalizes the disturbing truths and throws us a warning." Imagine how the world might be if more brands used this same approach in their advertising.

46 — Toscani, O. (1996). *Adiós a la Publicidad* (2nd ed.). Barcelona: Ediciones Omega.

Images can be used as weapons of communication in the fight against society's inequities. For this reason, Amnesty International has taken a similar approach to that employed by Benetton: straight-talking, hard-hitting campaigns that are real, violent and shocking for the eyes of those who live in peace. Some may say that these methods should not be used by those who promote the well-being of humanity. They may have a point, but these campaigns do raise awareness for the unbearable realities that exist in the world, and they may mobilize people to react to injustices.

To provide one example, together with the advertising agency Walker, Amnesty International Switzerland created a thought-provoking campaign on the subject of human rights abuses. Under the slogan "It's Not Happening Here. But It's Happening Now," a series of two hundred posters portrayed abuses as if they were happening in the streets of Switzerland by juxtaposing real pictures of human abuses with local background images.

Pius Walker, the campaign's art director, pointed out that "creating an advertising campaign for a sensitive subject is never easy. After all, no one wants to dramatize a drama. . . . What was needed here was the simplest truth being told in the simplest way. Something no one can argue with is harder to ignore."[47] The difficulty of ignoring such images was actually one of the agency's concerns, as the images had the potential to offend and

Oliviero Toscani: "Hearts," 1996. Campaign

scandalize sensitive passersby such as children and their parents.

47 — D&DA. (2006). "Case Study: Amnesty International. It's not Happening Here, but it's Happening Now," in *D&DA Impact*.

The campaign was a risky one. In the end, the posters were one of the most successful Amnesty International campaigns in Switzerland, and their impact spread to other parts of the world. People aren't used to seeing these types of images, and they may even feel offended because they don't want to imagine life outside of their comfort zone. The idea that people won't react, or that they will react negatively, isn't true, however. After all, who can be indifferent to the cruel and unfair reality facing other human beings?

Throughout history, things that represent breaks from the norm usually produce discomfort, which is probably one of the reasons why this approach works so well—when it is done appropriately. Just as in real life, when it comes to graphic design, we shouldn't always strive for happiness; sometimes it is better to aim for reality instead. It is important to note that scandalous design is not about inflicting pain but rather about acknowledging its presence.

walker.ag: "Not here but now," 2006. Posters and billboards

A graphic piece can relate to both the public and the designer simultaneously. When this happens, the design becomes a vehicle for sharing fun and enjoyable moments through a collaborative design process or through the final piece itself. Regardless of the stage of the process when it happens, the resulting designs bring out feelings of connectedness between their viewers and creators. If design can be a tool that helps in achieving personal goals—or even a time capsule that triggers past memories—it can create stronger bonds with the individual.

Who we are / Who we want to be

"Design creates culture. Culture shapes values. Values determine the future. Design is therefore responsible for the world our children will live in." —ROBERT L. PETERS

Achievements

As human beings, we surround ourselves with things that we believe will help us achieve personal goals or fulfil personal needs. Throughout our life, we search for items that will enhance our existence, and whatever allows us to carry out our ambitions will remain dear in our memory. In order to create similarly long-lasting emotional bonds between graphic design and its audience, design pieces should be complex enough to fulfil people's expectations. Provoking a burst of enthusiasm in people when they first see a design is important to get their attention, but it won't hold it over time. Graphic design should go beyond frivolity in order to help people achieve their personal goals and to "fulfil our social, cultural, and material needs for status and acceptance."[48]

48 — van Gorp, T., & Adams, E. *Op. cit.*

Designs can do this if they take the routine and turn it into a special experience. For example, the right design can make reading a newspaper be a more immersive experience than a simple process of ascertaining what events have recently taken place in the world, or it can make consulting a map feel more exciting than an act of seeking information. The job of graphic designers is to be innovative, original and sophisticated. We can come up with ways to make people believe that design can improve everyone's quality of life and to make ordinary actions extraordinary. One way to start doing these things is to think about our own profession: What can we do to improve our working processes and facilitate our tasks? If the solutions that we find can be adapted to other people's ways of working, we will go from helping a few to helping thousands. This was what happened with one of herraizsoto&co.'s projects. This Barcelona-based creative agency developed an app for use within the firm that would assist in the task of writing by hiding distractions and providing an inspirational interface.

Pleasantly surprised by the benefits of the tool, the agency decided to distribute it on the App Store (under the name OmmWriter) for others who need to escape from commonplace distractions. Based on the number of downloads (one million) and active users (half a million), it appears that this app meets many writers' needs. Advertised on OmmWriter's website as "a perfect place to think and write," the app provides users with natural backgrounds, audio tracks and typing sounds that boost creativity, improve concentration and let ideas flow naturally.

Since this app was meant for writing, I decided to give it a try and use it to write this book. While I write these words, I can hear the sound of

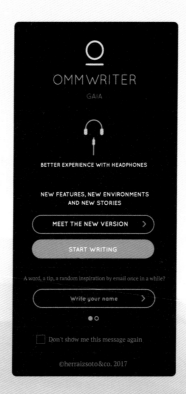

O

OMMWRITER

GAIA

BETTER EXPERIENCE WITH HEADPHONES

NEW FEATURES, NEW ENVIRONMENTS
AND NEW STORIES

MEET THE NEW VERSION >

START WRITING

A word, a tip, a random inspiration by email once in a while?

Write your name >

● ○

☐ Don't show me this message again

TYPEFACES THAT MAKE YOU WANT TO WRITE

—

Open Sans

ABCDEFGHIJKLMNOPQRSTUVWXYZ
abcdefghijklmnopqrstuvwxyz
0123456789(!@#$%&.,?:;)

Each text has its own personality and each writer his or her own style. From among a number of typefaces, choose the one which best suits your inspiration. From strong, solid fonts for those who know exactly what they want to say, to fonts that seem to paint your words as if a paintbrush were breathing life into them.

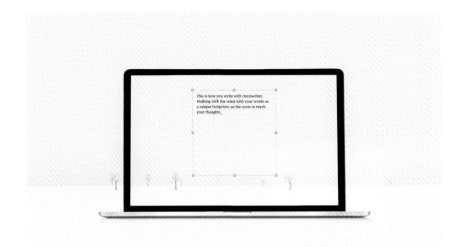

This is how you write with Ommwriter.
Walking with the wind with your words as
a unique footprints on the snow to reach
your thoughts_

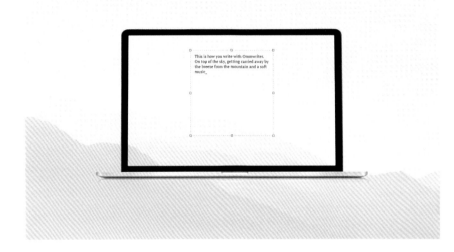

This is how you write with Ommwriter.
On top of the sky, getting carried away by
the breese from the mountain and a soft
music_

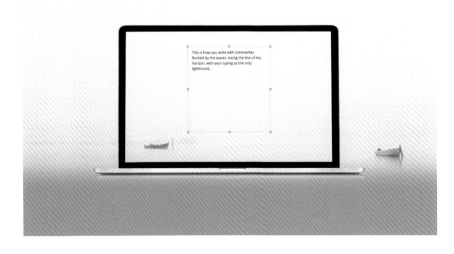

This is how you write with Ommwriter.
Rocked by the waves, losing the line of the
horizon, with your typing as the only
lighthouse_

waves and seagulls in what I presume to be a sunny day at the beach, which contrasts with a white winter setting in the app's background. Each key that I press creates a subtle sound mimicking old typewriters, and this is gratifying enough to keep me writing. I think the success of this tool lies in its simplicity, minimalism and full-screen mode. Once I begin typing, the (few) controls that allow me to change settings disappear, leaving me alone with my thoughts and words. This app is a clear example of a simple solution for a complex problem, namely how to simultaneously stay focused, relaxed and productive. It makes me realise that many apps and tools have actually been developed to help with multitasking, whereas OmmWriter succeeds in doing the exact opposite. In my opinion, herraizsoto&co. have done a great job of helping writers to achieve their creative goals by helping them to focus on only one task, which ultimately allows better results to be achieved.

In order to help people reach their personal goals, it is necessary to know what those goals are, or, in other words, what things our audience is trying to overcome. The key is to "capitalize on human strengths and encourage positive associations through clear goals, reduced distractions, immediate feedback and a sense of accomplishment."[49] This means designers should think big but start small, working with the wherewithal they have at hand. There is no need to help everyone at once, and it isn't possible to do so. Instead, we should approach each situation based on its specific characteristics and requirements. We might be pleasantly surprised to find later on that a solution or design suits a wider audience than first thought. This is exactly what happened in the case of a project developed by the entrepreneur ShaoLan.

49 — *Ibid.*

As a Taiwanese mother of children who were born and raised in the UK, ShaoLan found the task of teaching Chinese characters to her kids extremely challenging. This experience led her on a journey to find the easiest and most fun way to learn Chinese. On the way, ShaoLan devised a method to break down thousands of Chinese characters into simple "building blocks" that can then be reconstructed into more complex words. This way, the students—first her children, then a larger audience—could create multiple new words and sentences through knowing just a few building blocks. Roughly speaking, we can say it is based on the Pareto Principle, meaning that by mastering 20% of Chinese characters, the students will then be 80% fluent in Chinese. To make this method even more effective for a Western public, ShaoLan commissioned the illustrator Noma Bar to combine the meaning of the characters with

Rafa Soto

Creative director, co-founder of herraizsoto&co.

What does emotional design mean to you?

Well, we relate intimately to everything that surrounds us, and this affects us much more than we can imagine. Related to that, I think there is a lot of mimicry with what's around. For example, Gaudí made his houses with round corners because of the peace that this type of shape conveys. I know this is interior design and architecture, but hey, that's emotional design, right? There is osmosis between our emotions and what is outside. We don't decode it logically but emotionally. It has to do with shapes and colours, and how they affect us without us realizing it.

OmmWriter is a very simple writing tool with few controls. Do you get feedback asking to add more features? How do you balance users' demands with your vision for the product?

There is always a dichotomy between doing what people ask you to do and doing what you think you have to do. That is, what is your vision regarding the vision of the people? There are several experts in the field who have different opinions. Some will tell you that the product isn't yours, and if you think it is then you have no idea how to launch a product. On the other hand, other experts will say that if you do what people tell you, you will have a crappy product because they don't know what a good product is. I think that you have to find the midpoint between these two views: be flexible and do what people ask of you but without giving up the essence of the product.

In the case of OmmWriter, if we had listened to everything they asked of us, we would have ended up being something like Pages or Microsoft Word. However, we have found very interesting jewels in users' feedback. It made a lot of sense to give in sometimes. For example, some people asked us to include a monospaced font to write code. We thought it was so cool that people wanted to write code directly in OmmWriter that we included it.

Do you think graphic design can help people to achieve their life goals? Would you like to produce designs that do that?

Yes, we would love it! When you are a publicist—and although this is a stereotype, a big part of it is true—you dedicate yourself to deceiving people. Well, maybe not deceiving, but to showing them a very inspirational world they will never live in, or even if they do, a world that won't bring them happiness. There is a lot of speculation in the world of advertising. It always gives you a little bit of a feeling of not contributing much to society. You do not have any feedback from consumers either, as they are very far from you. On the other hand, when you launch a product and it works, people do send you feedback! With OmmWriter, we got some very special comments from a North American writer. She told us she had been having a creative block for over two years. Thanks to OmmWriter, she was able to get back to writing and couldn't stop doing it for forty-eight hours straight. Apparently, we gave her the greatest gift of her life. These things, as creatives, give much more meaning to what we do than when we do advertising. Because of this, the OmmWriter project was a bit cathartic to me because it made me think that I would rather be a creative person who brings something to people than one who adds even more noise to an already noisy society. Obviously graphic design can help me with that, because it is the skin—and often even the soul—of everything we do.

木 tree (mu[4])

The building block for 'tree' represents a tree trunk with hanging branches. When this character is used as an adjective, it refers to a wooden texture. When it is used to describe a person, it means 'clumsy', 'dumb' or 'numb'.

火 fire

月 moon

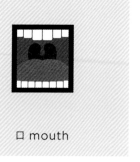

口 mouth

woods

forest

foundation

to come

林 woods (lin²)

Two trees together make a wood, which is greater than a single tree. This character is also a common surname, pronounced 'Lin'. It's actually my mother's surname.

森 forest (sen¹)

Three trees make a forest, which is greater than a tree or a wood. When used as an adjective, this character means 'dense', just like a thick cluster of trees.

本 foundation (ben³)

The foundation of a house is the first step in its construction, and traditionally foundations were made of wood. This character also means 'origin'.

來 to come (lai²)

This character is a combination of 'tree' and two 'person' building blocks. In ancient China, 'to come' was represented by a character based on wheat, which had been brought to China from Europe. The simplified form is 来.

人 person

女 woman

水 water

simple illustrations whose forms were based on the shape of the characters. Each character had to "look stunning" and be "stylistically consistent" and "educationally effective"[50] in order to engage the student to learn more and more blocks. With hard work and a sense of humour, Chineasy—an easy and funny illustrated method to learn Chinese—was born.

"It is educational, social, cultural, and I hope, inspirational," ShaoLan told *dezeen* magazine.[51] With the help of a Kickstarter campaign, she managed to create a set of educational tools— books, mobile apps, board games and flash- cards—that both teach the language and educate users about the cultural and historical influences behind the vocabulary. ShaoLan's personal goal is to bridge the gap between the East and West, which exists in part due to the difficulties that Westerners experience when they attempt to memorize and understand the complexity of the Chinese language. ShaoLan believes that through Chineasy she can contribute to shaping society: "Whilst the entire Chinese population is learning English, it is time for us to really comprehend this complex economy and society with our own eyes, knowledge and judgment."[52] The project won the Wallpaper* Design Award's 2014 Life-Enhancer of the Year, which demonstrates its success in extending and enhancing people's cognitive capabilities.

Both of the examples presented here offer benefits to their own target markets, and also, at a deeper level, to society as a whole. They take simple problems, needs and desires faced by the audience and design solutions for them. Needless to say, the outcomes of contributing to people's success are most likely positive. In the same way that we feel thankful when some- one helps us with a big task, a graphic design that helps will also trigger strong positive emotions within the public. The designer and writer Frank Chimero said something interesting in his book *The Shape of Design* that I think applies in this context: "Design's middle position requires it to aid movement in both directions. The most useful bridges, after all, allow traffic to go both ways."[53] From this point of view, both designer and viewer will benefit from a piece that is valued as contributing to personal goals and well-being. Emotions come and go, allowing people on both ends of the bridge to embrace them.

50 — ShaoLan. (2013). "Chineasy: The easiest way to learn Chinese." Retrieved (November 18, 2017) from: https://www.kickstarter.com/proj- ects/shaolanchineasy/chineasy-be- gins-0/description

51 — Griffiths, A. (2014, April). "Chineasy illustrated characters designed to make learning Chinese easy," in *Dezeen Magazine*. Re- trieved from: https://www.dezeen. com/2014/04/12/chineasy-illustrat- ed-characters-learning-chinese-no- ma-bar/

52 — ShaoLan. *Op. cit.*

53 — Chimero, F. (2012). *The Shape of Design*. (M. Brown, Ed.) (1st ed.). Minnesota: Shapco Printing.

Memories

Triggering memories is not something that designers can completely control. What we can do is design devices that attempt to prompt viewers to recall previous experiences. This experience could be a long-forgotten event from their childhood, or simply a meeting with friends the week before. These recollections can work as powerful triggers of long-lasting emotions as long as viewers feel that there is a real connection between the design and their identity.

Powerful memories sometimes cause graphic pieces that were meant to be disposable—for instance, concert tickets or event flyers—to be preserved with care as part of a collection of mementos. If an event brings happiness to someone, that person will likely want to keep a visual and tactile memory of that happy time. Unfortunately, in the case of concert tickets, the design chosen is not always an interesting one. In fact, tickets are often the same for every concert and are based on a model that is designed by the company responsible for selling the tickets. So why not design beautiful and engaging products that would bring an even greater desire for the owner to keep them, not only because of the memories they trigger but also because of their appealing design?

What if, as designers, we really want to trigger memories for the viewer? Thinking about our own childhoods is probably the most straightforward starting point. After all, our childhood memories—such as the toys we played with, the cartoons we watched and the activities we took part in—don't differ from one person to another a great deal. Just think of a game you played at a young age. In my case, many of my friends played the same game. All of us can surely remember enjoyable times spent playing as children. When a graphic piece evokes experiences similar to the ones we had back then—to which we are already strongly connected—we'll most likely experience the same emotions we felt previously. Brosmind provides a prime example of this premise in action. Juan and Alejandro Mingarro are the two brothers behind this Barcelona-based illustration studio, and they believe that their initial references from childhood—action figures, adventure films and comic books from the 1980s and 1990s—are the seeds of their work: "We have always believed that our current style has in some way been influenced by pop culture from that time period, not so much aesthetically, but in the sense of wonder that pervaded during this unforgettable time."[54]

54 — Brosmind. (2014). *Why, How, What* (1st ed.). Barcelona: Norma Editorial.

The Brosmind brothers have always been a team. From an early age, they created their own action figures and comic books to complement their limited collections of official entertainment merchandising (including that from *Teenage Mutant Ninja Turtles, Ghostbusters, Masters of the Universe* and Marvel comics, among others). The studio now uses these nostalgic memories as a source of inspiration. The *Brosmind Crime* series is just one example where characters from 1980s pop culture were brought to the present, but with an added twist in the form of Brosmind's current graphic style. This series was in fact an attempt for the two brothers to toughen their cheerful style by creating an array of evil characters that can be paired with cartoon villains from our childhood. The shapes and colour palettes, however, make these illustrations impossible to be mistaken for another artist's work. Some of the characters from the *Brosmind Crime* project were also further developed. For example, Olfato Mike's backstory is told through an old-fashioned radio broadcast recorded on vinyl—just in case you didn't feel nostalgic already.

Heroes and villains are not the only characters present in the Brosmind universe. *Unicorn*—which the studio considers to be one of the most complex and unique pieces that it's ever made—depicts one of the charming French-style carousels that delight children all over the world. Although the unicorn was reinterpreted according to Brosmind's distinctive whimsical style, it still draws memories from the viewer, allowing the studio to better connect with its audience.

Evoking memories is about using a shared language based on mutual cultural experiences. For example, how many of us ever went to funfairs, or drew the route out of a maze printed in the puzzles section of a magazine, or played spot the difference?

The French digital print designer Camille Walala took all of these activities and mixed them into a colourful and playful installation at NOW Gallery in London. "WALALA x PLAY" consists of a maze whose walls reflect vivid patterns in bold colours. By placing mirrors strategically and making subtle changes to the patterns, Walala invites visitors to explore the colours, shapes and scales in order to identify the inconsistencies between two otherwise identical surfaces. In order to complete this "task," visitors are encouraged to play and physically interact with the environment. NOW Gallery states that "Walala has set out to create a temple to wonder in which visitors can unleash their inner child and lose themselves in colour and pattern."[55] At a 2018 OFFF talk in Barcelona, the artist herself commented that she was surprised by the success of the installation and

Brosmind: "Unicorn," 2009–13. Sculpture

‹

was touched by the fact that visitors came to thank her for making them "feel like a child again."

If something as simple as a playground triggers such strong emotions for the audience, we can infer that there is little point in using obscure ideas that are unlikely to be identified by the public. If the objective of graphic design is to communicate a message in a way that the audience will understand, we should leverage how people naturally make sense of new information. Throughout our lives, we collect experiences that we then reflect upon when we face a new situation in an attempt to better understand it. As designers we can make this task easier for our audience by guiding them to the exact experience and memory we want them to recall. Naturally, we are unable to target—at least intentionally—very personal memories. Instead, we can think of common memories that are more likely to be shared. By knowing our public better, we will be better prepared to tap into memories that will help the creative process and connect with people at a deeper level.

55 — Morby, A. (2017, July). "Camille Walala creates colourful labyrinth inside London's Now Gallery," in *Dezeen*. Retrieved from: https://www.dezeen.com/2017/07/13/camille-walala-creates-colourful-labyrinth-inside-london-now-gallery-installation-design/

Cocreation

Cocreation has a lot to do with self-image, which is known to play an important role in people's lives and everyday actions. For example, any material possession or behaviour amounts to a public expression of ourselves, and most of us care in some way or another about how we are perceived by others. Equally, any design piece that represents the personality of the designer's audience and matches that personality with the designer's or the client's will forge a deeper relationship between them all, promoting brand loyalty.

Participative creation is a straightforward way of ending up with a project that the public can relate to. Designers can learn about the public's needs and desires by getting it involved in their projects from the beginning. This practice will allow the designer to understand the practical and emotional benefits that the audience hoped to obtain from a graphic piece, thus providing the basis to design it accordingly.

An example of how designers can put this principle into practice can be seen in the #monologueando campaign, which was directed by the Barcelona-based studio THIS is UMAMI for the wine label Monólogo. This

Camille Walala: "WALALA X PLAY," 2017. Installation at Now Gallery, London

studio bases projects on three frameworks, one of which they call Fando-making. This name comes from the acknowledgment that fandoms—that is, communities of fans—are willing to do anything for the subject of their admiration. THIS is UMAMI tries "to give the audience … the role of actors in communication through collective creations."[56]

For this project, the studio launched a campaign on Twitter inviting Monólogo's fans to share monologues under the hashtag #mono-logueando. With thousands of responses submitted, 150 of these thoughts, ideas and perspectives on life were chosen to be part of the brand's communication campaign. The chosen submissions were typographically illustrated in colourful graphics and later published in book that came in online and offline versions and was entirely written by Monólogo's customers. If we look more closely, we can see that the studio's approach was actually very simple: "Listen carefully to what the fans of the brand want to tell us."[57] This campaign not only engaged the public but also acknowledged its importance, and this was reinforced through limited-edition bottles that featured three of the chosen monologues on the label. Due to the huge success of the campaign, the same approach was used again the following year, and a collaborative summer hit for Monólogo and its fans was born.

Let's now shift out attention to the exchange of information between people. Humans make raw data intelligible by processing and interpreting it. Through this process, we create information. However, even if a person has a cognitive understanding of a piece of information, he or she may not grasp why it is meaningful or important. And although infographics are becoming increasingly sophisticated, on their own they can struggle to communicate information in a way that is meaningful on an emotional level

Domestic Data Streamers (DDS) found a solution for this issue. The mission of the Barcelona-based studio is to "communicate through data storytelling by bringing emotions to data, simplifying complex information and generating knowledge." By replacing common infographics with collaborative info-experiences, DDS aspires to empower viewers/participants with data that means something to them and that they can relate to.[58]

One such example is the Data Strings installation that DDS presented at SWAB International Contemporary Art Fair. The installation consisted of a set of personal questions and

56 — THIS is UMAMI. (n.d.). "About." Retrieved (October 15, 2016) from: http://thisisumami.com/about/

57 — THIS is UMAMI. (2016). "#Mono-logueando Campaign." Retrieved (October 15, 2016) from: http://thisisumami.com/project/monolo-go-monologueando-campaign/

58 — García, P. (2015). "Data, art and new ways of understanding the world." TEDxBarcelona. Retrieved from: https://www.youtube.com/watch?v=9XgXZMoH1Jw

THIS is UMAMI: "#monologueando," 2016. Campaign and wine labels

possible answers to them that was placed on a matrix across a wall. Participants were asked to answer the questions by running string through the matrix. They therefore shaped the information displayed in a way that allowed them to see themselves reflected in it. The end result was a large-scale infographic that changed the way in which people looked at things and interacted with each other. The matrix's versatility led to the installation of Data Strings at several venues and events, which in itself generated new conversations and discussions. For the DDS team, the key point of this project was to allow participants to see their own story: "When you can visualise and express what you are thinking, it becomes a bigger and more important story."[59] In situ participation is not the only way to adopt the cocreation principle. DDS had also designed projects where online participation was enough to give the public a feeling of collaboration. The Nike iD Website, for instance, is a tool developed for Air Max Day, through which customers could customize a pair of these iconic shoes based on what they hoped to accomplish with them. The platform asked users three questions, and each response modified the design of one part of the shoe. The questions were "What are you doing?" for the body; "From where to where?" for the sole; and "Why?" for the laces. Each buyer would then receive a unique and personalized pair of shoes, created according to their goals.

What we can learn from these projects is that people have very interesting things to say, and their participation can be crucial to the success of a design piece or campaign. It is normal for designers to sometimes be stuck with a project and to not know where to begin. In an attempt to overcome this feeling, we could begin by asking the people that we're designing for about their expectations and opinions. We can ask them to help us visualize the information that we want to communicate and give them an important role in the overall process. The advantages of this method are often surprising and lead to a final design that is both appealing and intelligent.

59 — Domestic Data Streamers. (2015). "East Meets West." Retrieved (March 16, 2017) from: http://domesticstreamers.com/case-study/data-strings/

Domestic Data Streamers: "Data Strings," 2014. Participative installation

EAST
MEETS
WEST

Where are you from?
你的居住地

Locals
香港

Asia
亞洲

Rest of the World
世界其他地區

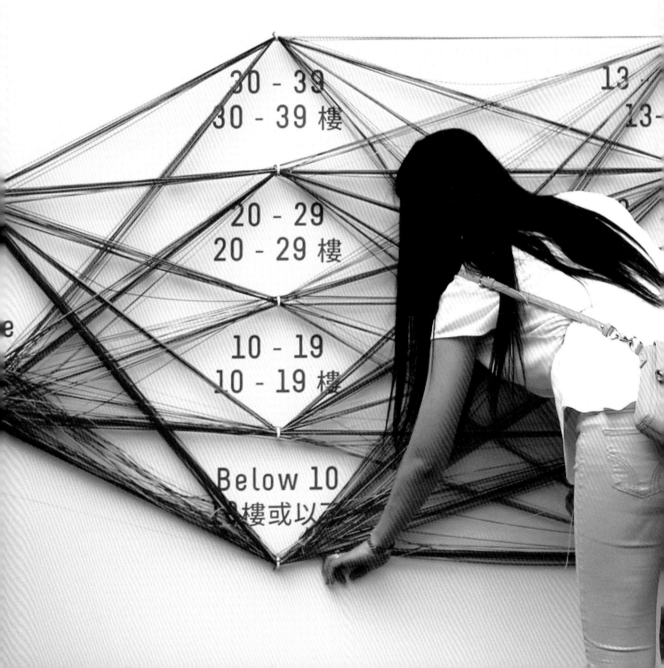

Humour

Paula Scher, a partner at Pentagram, once said, "You have to be in a state of play to design. If you're not in a state of play you can't make anything."[60] This quote should be displayed on the walls of every design agency and studio around the globe. If a designer has fun creating, improvising and trying new things, the results will undoubtedly mirror this "state of play" and engage viewers. A playful design—one that uses humorous language, that surprises the public and that entices their creativity—is more likely to prompt a strong emotional reaction and increase emotional well-being and creativity, both for the creator and for the audience. Laughter causes viewers to drop their guard, allowing them to become more receptive to the message that is being communicated and, in turn, more receptive to new ideas and perspectives.

As designers and creators, we should explore approaches that let us produce better human interactions between the viewer and our creation. Such interactions can be generated by sharing our sense of humour, which will reveal our true values and allow a more authentic and profound connection with our audience. We can think about a time when we intentionally made someone laugh and wonder how this experience affected our relationship with that person and what feelings came out of that interaction. The use of humour may also encourage people to take a closer look at the message and to pay more attention to what is being said; if they do these things, communication will have been meaningful and successful.

There are no rules on how to design with humour. However, a joke is only valid in a certain context, and whether or not people will appreciate it depends on how well it fits within that context. It is important to consider the demographic and psychographic backgrounds of the audience and to engage its members' senses of humour. If we can't make our public laugh, do we know who we are designing for? One thing is for sure: laughter is universal, and its benefits have been studied for quite a long time. Whether it relieves stress or dull pain, humour creates social bonds that will almost certainly be beneficial for the relationship between designers and their audiences. Nevertheless, we should be careful not to force a laugh. People will likely notice it and may perceive the design as untrustworthy. If you think your sense of humour is not your best asset, maybe going for a different approach would be the best option.

60 — Netflix. (2017). "Abstract: The Art of Design. Paula Scher." Episode 6. Retrieved (September 3, 2018) from: https://vimeo.com/210061645

Erika Zorzi and Matteo Sangalli certainly don't lack a sense of humour. This duo behind the New York-based studio Mathery focus their work on photography, film direction, installation and set design to create pieces that display "hints of an eccentric and romantic ideal."[61] I first came across their work when I was attending the 2018 design and innovation festival OFFF, which takes place annually in Barcelona. Mathery was commissioned to create the festival campaign and opening film, and the studio did so with a playful mindset and a dose of surrealism.

OFFF started in 2001 as the Online Flash Film Festival. Over the years, it has evolved into a more extensive event, and the acronym has lost meaning to the point where, by its eighteenth edition, no one had a clue about what each letter of OFFF represented. Mathery studio found this fact very interesting and decided to base the festival campaign on it: "We thought it would be a really fun opportunity to come out with a narrative idea behind a name of four letters, and go crazy with that."[62] And crazy they went! By mixing Mathery's sense of humour, some absurd thoughts and vivid colours, OFFF was translated into eight different nonsensical festivals, such as the "Ornamental Flying Frogs Festival" or the "Orthopedic Floral Footwear Festival." These alternative festivals were shown in photographic narratives and used to promote the real OFFF festival.

Another way to depict humour is to incorporate playfulness into graphic pieces. For example, puzzles, charades, and not-so-straightforward jokes have the potential to engage viewers as they figure out what the design is about. The moment the viewers get the joke or solve the puzzle, they will feel triumphant and remember the design fondly.

Does a poster that features a black background, an eye, a bee and the letter M ring a bell? You may remember it, or at least have heard of its designer. If you're thinking about Paul Rand, you're absolutely right. In fact, his distinctive sense of play has led him to be considered one of the best graphic designers who ever lived.

Although styles and trends have changed since Rand's day, his pieces are still appreciated today, mostly because of their interesting compositions and childlike wit. The aforementioned IBM (eye-bee-M) poster is one of those timeless pieces that intrigues the public by making people feel that there's something to unravel. Rand used the rebus as a communication

61 — Mathery. (n.d.). *About. Mathery.* Retrieved (May 25, 2018) from: http://mathery.it/about

62 — TRUST Collective. (2018). "1stAveMachine Directing Duo Mathery Brings Playful Perspective to An Ambiguous Acronym for OFFF Barcelona 2018 Promo." Retrieved (June 2, 2018) from: https://www.trustcollective.com/2018/05/08/1stavemachine-directing-duo-mathery-offers-surreal-colorful-glimpse-before-the-show-in-offf-barcelona-2018-teaser/

Mathery Studio: "OFFF Barcelona," 2018. Graphic and visual campaign

Ornamental Flying Frogs Festival

Orange Fringed Fathers Festival

Optimistic Freckled Friends Festival

Oily Furry Fingers Festival

Overdressed Ferocious Faces Festival

Orthopedic Floral Footwear Festival

Oysters Flavoured Food Festival

Oversensitive French Fiancées Festival

tool, and he believed it to be both informative and entertaining. In the book *Thoughts on Design*, Rand criticizes people who believe graphic design must deploy a sober communicative approach. He argued that "the notion that the humorous approach to visual communication is undignified or belittling is sheer nonsense" and that by "means of juxtaposition, association, size, relationship, proportion, space or special handling,"[63] a designer is able to create unforgettable humorous pieces.

63 — Rand, P. (1970) *Thoughts on Design*. (third). New York: Studio Vista/ Van Nostrand Reinhold.

However, it is advisable to use humour carefully, and not to let a joke distract the viewer from the design's main objective. Instead, humour should be the component that takes a visual message from being informative to being enjoyable. Studies reveal that a good sense of humour is a sign of intelligence, as it "helps us determine whether or not the information we receive from our senses is logical and meaningful."[64] I truly believe that fun graphic design is a worthwhile pursuit. If life becomes easier when we laugh about it, why shouldn't this also be the case when it comes to graphic design?

64 — Bradley, H. (2015). *Design Funny: The Graphic Designer's Guide to Humor*. (Scott Francis, Ed.). Cincinnati: HOW Books.

Paul Rand

Graphic designer

"The Role of Humour"

Readership surveys demonstrate the significance of humour in the field of visual communication. The reference is not principally to cartoon strip advertisements or to out-and-out gags, but to a subtler variety, one indigenous to the design itself and achieved by means of association, juxtaposition, size relationship, proportion, space or special handling.

The visual message that professes to be profound or elegant often boomerangs as mere pretension; and the frame of mind that looks at humour as trivial and flighty mistakes the shadow for the substance. In short, the notion that the humorous approach to visual communication is undignified or belittling is sheer nonsense. This misconception has been discredited by those entrepreneurs who have successfully exploited humour as a means of creating confidence, goodwill and a receptive frame of mind toward an idea or product. Radio and television commercials have made tremendous strides in the use of humour as a potent sales device. And, as an aid to understanding serious problems in war training, as an effective weapon in safety posters, war bond selling and morale building, humour was neglected by neither government nor civilian agencies in time of war.

Stressing the profound effects of entertainment, Plato, in *The Republic*, declares: "Therefore do not use compulsion, but let early education be rather a sort of amusement." The arts of ancient China, India and Persia reflect a humorous spirit in the design of masks, ceramics and paintings. American advertising in its infancy also demonstrated this tendency toward humour in, for example, the cigar store Indian and the medicine man. That humour is a product of serious contemporary thought is revealed in the significant paintings and sculptures by, for instance, Picasso, Miró, Ernst, Duchamp, Dubuffet. "True humour," says Thomas Carlyle, "springs not more from the head than from the heart; it is not contempt, its essence is love, it issues not in laughter but in still smiles, which lie far deeper."

Extracted from Rand, P. (1970). *Thoughts on Design* (third). New York: Studio Vista van Nostrand Reinhold.

Paul Rand: "Sources and Resources of 20th Century Design," 1966. Poster. Museum of Modern Art (MoMA). Offset lithograph 24 x 30 1/2' Gift of the artist 496.1978

Sources and Resources
of 20th Century Design

June 19 to 24, 1966
The International Design
Conference in Aspen

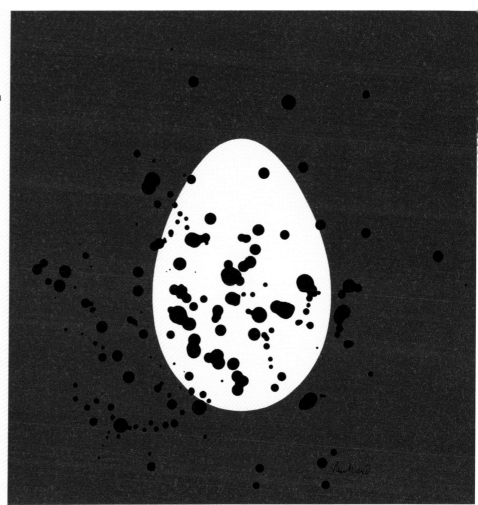

an Eye   for perception, insight, vision.
a Bee   for industriousness, dedication, perseverance.
an "M" for motivation, merit, moral strength.

A somewhat unusual perspective of the familiar
IBM logotype, and a light reminder of some of the fundamental qualities that have come to characterize
the outstanding men and women who have built, and who
continue to build, the success of the IBM company.

Our audience is made of human beings who are just like us. We all learn and experience things throughout our lives that define and shape our understanding of the world. If a design manages to question or counter these already formed ideas and beliefs by showing different perspectives, it will certainly impact those who see it.

Standards

"I believe that the weapon of the designer is the graphic consolidation of thoughts and must be used with a purpose. My pencil-rifle is not a weapon to kill, but to shoot the consciences through graphic language."
—ISIDRO FERRER

Understanding

The most important lesson to take from the principle of understanding is that our public is made up of people like us. They may have different life-styles, expectations and perspectives on life. However, everybody wants to be treated like a real person with real feelings rather than merely being the target of a communication campaign.

This communication is possible with an emotion-driven design—a design that expresses and understands the emotions of the audience. There's no need to develop spectacular insights about people, or to focus on rare capabilities that only apply to a small proportion of the population. We can, of course, take these things into consideration, but we should also be interested in the not so spectacular commonplace activities that are directly linked to our everyday lives. As Patrick W. Jordan argues, "Looking at people merely as 'users' may create a paradigm in which the person is seen merely as a component within a working system—such approaches are 'dehumanising,' ignoring, as they tend to do, the very factors that make people human—for example, their hopes, fears, dreams, aspirations, principles and tastes."[65]

65 — W. Jordan, P. *Op. cit.*

There are simple things that make us human: our imperfections, our multiple individualities, and our fears and expectations. Yet these are often undervalued in graphic campaigns, which tend to focus instead on communicating perfect messages to a perfect crowd. Real people aren't perfect, and neither are designers or clients. So why not embrace that imperfection in our work and create real human connections with the public? As designers, we don't have to base our projects on fantastic concepts. Instead, we can build from genuine stories that are widely relatable.

This leads me to highlight a growing concern of mine: designers who try to make themselves fit a preconceived idea of what a designer should be. We increasingly see work that looks as though it has been designed to impress peers, to look good in a portfolio or even to win design awards, rather than to address a real public or to tell us something about its creator. Although these pieces are perfectly crafted, they end up looking the same, as if they had been created by the same person.

The North American graphic designer James Victore, whose mantra is "feck perfuction," believes that we should fight back against this lack of personality in design by exposing more of ourselves in our work. According to Victore, "There is a public out there thirsting—dying—for human

Adam J. Kurtz: *Things Are What You Make of Them*, 2017. Excerpts from the book. Penguin Random House, 2017

〉

HOW TO BEGIN AGAIN

- DON'T LOOK BACK IN ANGER
- CHECK YOUR PULSE
- DO YOUR RESEARCH
- RETOOL YOUR PRACTICE
- BE ACCOUNTABLE
- WRITE YOUR MANIFESTO
- DISAPPEAR (WITH INTENT)
- CHARGE FORWARD

HOW TO BE ~~HAPPY~~ HAPPIER

- EMBRACE YOURSELF
- ACKNOWLEDGE THE SAD
- CREATE & MEET GOALS
- FIND FRESH INSPIRATION
- SUNSHINE & RAINBOWS
- CELEBRATE EVERYTHING
- FEEL CONTENT
- FORGET THE "DESTINATION"

RAISE EACH OTHER UP

YOU ARE ON YOUR OWN
JOURNEY, BUT YOU ARE NOT
ALONE. EACH OF US IS
FIGHTING TO BE HEARD IN
A CHORUS OF OVERLAPPING
& INTERSECTING VOICES.
SUPPORT EACH OTHER'S
WORK, WORDS, PROJECTS
& PRODUCTS. WE ALL WIN
WHEN WE HELP EACH
OTHER SUCCEED.

EMBRACE YOURSELF

LIFE IS CONSTANTLY
REMINDING US ABOUT
WHAT WE DON'T HAVE, BUT
WHAT ABOUT ALL THAT WE
DO HAVE? WHAT MAKES
YOU SPECIAL? WHAT DO
YOU HAVE TO OFFER THE
WORLD AROUND YOU? WHAT
DO YOU ENJOY? FIND THE
THINGS THAT YOU DO LOVE
ABOUT YOURSELF.
THEY'RE ENOUGH.

contact, for a real, honest opinion. And that somebody else besides them 'gets it' and cares."[66] This is exactly how I feel when I look at the work of the NYC-based artist and designer Adam J. Kurtz, whose hand-written thoughts and doodles resonate with my own life and struggles.

In an interview with *Refinery29*, Kurtz stated that most of his challenges "weren't actually unique at all, but commonly shared anxieties, fears, and stresses that all types of people shared."[67] This realization led him to use his visual voice to establish a conversation with the audience, in which being honest and *real* allows him to be emotive and tackle difficult topics—for example, a lack of motivation, insecurity, women and LGBTQ rights, and love. Others can then draw on that voice as they communicate equally difficult sentiments. Through interactive journals, gift products, stationery, books and social media posts, Kurtz shares his advice on how we can live a happier life by being less hard on ourselves and others.

One example of this kind of work is the pocket-sized book *Things Are What You Make of Them: Life Advice for Creatives*, a compilation of Kurtz's advice, thoughts and essays that offers empathy and inspiration for creatives of all kinds and in any career path. The entire book has perforated pages so that readers can tear out their favourites and share or frame Kurtz's kind and empowering words, rendered in the artist's classic style. Described on the *Man Repeller* blog as "highly relatable,"[68] this book transfers the artist's energy onto the paper, presenting the public with a person who is also trying to belong in society while dealing with his own imperfections.

To quote James Victore once again, "As a graphic designer, if you do a good job of telling your own story, putting your experience, your knowledge, and your life into your work, it will resonate with your audience."[69] The fact that people will understand you better and connect at a higher level with the designed work makes being more open and vulnerable worthwhile.

Another way to be emotionally involved in the life of our audiences and create understanding and more human graphic pieces is to put ourselves in their shoes. By doing so, we'll not only better empathize with them but also develop meaningful goals for the project. Ruedi Baur, a Parisian graphic designer, calls this method "civic design" or "context design."[70] Each graphic project is born within

66 — Victore, J. (2010). *Victore or, Who Died and Made You Boss?* New York: Abrams.

67 — Ohikuare, J. (2017, October). "How To Stop Worrying And Slay Your Workdays." in *Refinery29*. Retrieved from https://www.refinery29.com/en-us/things-are-what-you-make-of-them-excerpt-adam-kurtz)

68 — Nahman, H. (2018, January). "MR Book Club: 10 Books the Team Is Learning From Right Now," in *Man Repeller*.

69 — Victore, J. *Op. cit.*

Adam J. Kurtz: *Things Are What You Make of Them*, 2017. Excerpts from the book. Penguin Random House, 2017

a context, and ignoring these conditions is not in the designer's or the public's best interests.

70 — Baur, R. (2016). Ruedi Baur lecture. Barcelona: Elisava. Retrieved from: https://vimeo.com/165037425

At his studio Intégral, Ruedi Baur specializes in developing signage for cultural and public institutions such as museums and universities. Since these are institutions where many people from different cultures and with different physical conditions gather, Baur faces the challenge of creating universal work that is also in harmony with the identity of the institution.

Amongst Intégral's projects, one in particular caught my attention. Together with the company EO-Guidage, Baur developed modular and adaptable signage that aims to be universally accessible. When I visit museums, I sometimes wonder how people with physical disabilities that restrict their senses or movements manage to find their way around. The accessible signage developed by Intégral tackles this question and provides several solutions. First of all, its position is accessible to someone who is either standing or sitting. The signs are printed on three-dimensional blocks that feature either a Braille description or a button that activates a spoken message, allowing for better information delivery and navigation of the site. Additionally, someone with a low level of literacy can easily understand the directions provided due to the inclusion of clear pictograms and universal symbols.

When it comes to universality and the concept of imperfection that I spoke of earlier in this chapter, Baur has an interesting theory that I would like to share. "To conceive of accessibility," he says, "is to think of the multiple, the different, the all-world, the contextual too, for never a single solution will answer all the problems, it will never be totally universal, never totally perfect."[71] Maybe designers shouldn't focus so much on creating ideal or flawless works, but rather on striving for authenticity, acknowledging the imperfect creatures that we all are.

71 — Baur, R. (2014). Intégral Ruedi Baur Paris. Retrieved (February 23, 2017) from: http://www.irb-paris.eu/projet/index/id/129

Intégral Ruedi Baur Paris and EO-Guidage: "Une gamme de signalétique accessible," 2014. Signage system

⟩

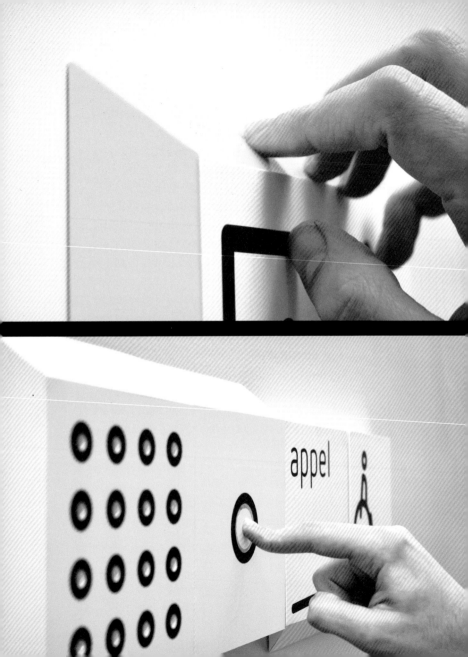

intégral → **eo** → → une gamme modulaire de signalétique [305] [306] conçue par ruedi baur. elle intègre les besoins liés à l'accessibilité pour tous et répond [210] Service aux besoins variés d'un social entrez bâtiment public. elle pourra [107] s'adapter en fonction des lieux.

Surprise

As creators, we often hear about magical and immediate reactions to a design piece. This is called the "wow factor." However, what this term means and what it represents aren't necessarily straightforward matters. Fortunately, some theorists have explained that there is no secret formula, and that the *"wow"* can be described as fascination, a pleasant surprise or a desire. This desire and fascination are caused by the curiosity that people feel when looking at the design and by the sudden and unexpected elements within the design itself.

As humans, we are programmed to like surprises. Our brains are always unconsciously seeking things that will make us feel motivated and that will break us out of the banality of everyday life. The more unpredictable the arrival of information to our brain is, the more addictive this feeling becomes. Studies on the area show that surprise can elicit many other kinds of emotions.[72] However, the more positive the surprise is, the more pleasant and memorable the experience of interacting with a design will be.

In line with this idea, unusual things tend to make a strong impression. The experience

72 — Bisquerra, R. *Op. cit.*

is enhanced if this impression is something that the audience can recall as being uplifting and delightful. Let's look at the Science and Technology Park of University of Porto's (UPTEC) signage system, designed by the creative studio Claan, as an example. UPTEC is a space that brings together academic knowledge and business know-how in promoting local entrepreneurship. In 2012, UPTEC opened the Innovation Centre, where projects at the forefront of technological and scientific innovation are developed.

Despite the high level of creativity and novelty coming out of the Innovation Centre's labs, the building itself didn't reflect these activities. Clara Vieira, cofounder of the Porto-based studio Claan, described the place as "dead, totally inexpressive and uncomfortable." This ambience, she believed, limited the creativity of the people who worked there. The client came to Claan asking for signage that communicated UPTEC's values and mirrored the cutting-edge technology that it was hosting.

The result was a set of giant graphics that invaded the previously inhospitable space and created optical illusions through anamorphic typography. If the fact that these graphics were huge—covering entire doors and corridors—wasn't enough to surprise the viewer, the distortions gave the final unexpected and innovative touches that UPTEC needed. The signage system's main attraction is the seven-metre-long anamorphic numbers

Clara Vieira and Andreas Eberharter

Graphic designers, co-founders of Claan

Which attitudes, processes and decisions allow you to design something that engages the public emotionally?

Andreas Eberharter (AE): First of all, we somehow select the projects on which we work. Why? Because we must identify with the project itself. Otherwise the result may be affected. Once we start working on those projects, we always try to go a little bit beyond the initial briefing.

Clara Vieira (CV): This approach lets us have a personal involvement in the project, and, therefore, we can reflect our emotional perspective through the graphic style.

AE: Our emotional approach also depends on the project. As an example, designing a graphic identity is completely different to designing a mobile app. However, we always focus on the users, meaning that we try to support the tasks and actions they want to do. It is when we mix this support with visual communication—as in, the branding and graphic brief that we must follow—that we make it personal. It is easier to reach users through emotional tools; we go beyond the filter of the rational and establish a direct connection with them. If designers want to accomplish that using only intellectual tools, we need to come up with a really good concept and give time to the user to understand it fully. Emotional design is a shortcut.

CV: It is all about the affinity we have with the recipient of our design.

What does emotional design mean to you?

CV: The term isn't new for us. We heard it first in Norman's book *Emotional Design*, in which the author points out the affinity with aesthetics and humour that a piece can have, which brings the user closer to that piece (even if it underperforms somehow). Apart from this, emotional design is present in our work process because of storytelling, and the ways we tell stories.

AE: After Norman came Jony Ive, who was also an inspiration for us.

CV: He talked about doing things with love, which would then be reflected in the final result. This is also a way to achieve an emotional graphic design: caring about it.

AE: I believe that when we show our own will and thoughts on the design, the public can relate to that later.

Do you think it is important to avoid clichés when you face a new project? What do you do to innovate in terms of the ways in which you communicate a message?

CV: Yes, for sure it is important to avoid clichés. However, I think it is something that comes naturally rather than a relentless search for the next new thing. Maybe we just try to think differently.

AE: It is also interesting to have a team made up of people from different countries and backgrounds. That is why we not only work with designers but also architects, industrial designers or developers. It isn't always easy to think of a new way, a new discourse and a new message every time we have a project. But we clearly have high goals in mind.

CV: The client needs to be involved and to give us space for experimentation. That happened on this project [UPTEC signage]; the client trusted us. And trust is the key for surprising results. Also, when there's trust, the responsibility to make something good is higher.

AE: Innovating means our being surrounded by a constellation surrounding us: made up of the client, trust, freedom and a multidisciplinary team. And also a willingness to experiment!

Claan: "Signage and Wayfinding for Innovation Center," 2013. Signage system

⟩

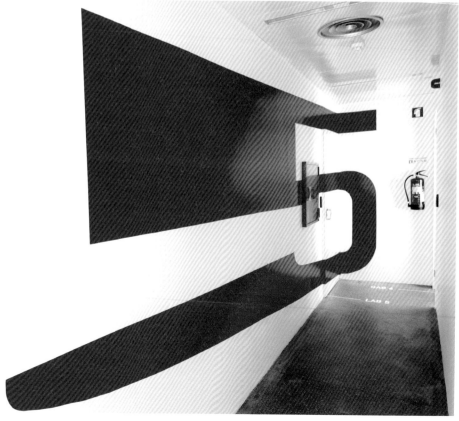

spread throughout the corridors. These numbers inform visitors of their location, guide them around the building and restrict entry to the labs. In addition to the navigational elements, a series of surprising features are integrated throughout the building, from inspirational sentences in bathrooms to an entire wall covered in post-it notes inside the "playground" common area.

In the end, any doubts raised by UPTEC's administrative board about whether the design would be too disruptive were withdrawn. This project worked as a strong statement for UPTEC and put it on the map, communicating to a broader audience about the work that was taking place at the University of Porto. Specialized books and magazines—for example, the *Graphic Design Annual 2014* by *Computer Arts*—praised the signage as an inspiring solution that made a strong impression. According to Claan, this project expands beyond the limits of perception and architecture, and it transforms the building into an object of interactive communication, which in turn facilitates interactions between UPTEC's workers.

To create a wow factor and make a design memorable, Andreas Eberharter (cofounder of Claan) says that "we need to be willing to experiment and not fear failure." Designers are capable of creating unusual things that depart from the norm, but only if we are ready to fail time and time again until we finally get it right. In my opinion, this process is a worthwhile pursuit, as it will bring new experiences not only for the public but also for the designers themselves.

Designs that elicit surprise usually try to cause a dynamic response in the eye of the viewer by using visually interactive techniques. Surprise can be triggered by new and unexpected stimuli, by interruptions or by sudden changes. It's all about defying our knowledge and expectations, delivering content in the wrong format. By "wrong," I mean something that our understanding of the world tells us is impossible. Let's take M. C. Escher as an example. Before graphic design was even a concept, this artist was experimenting with bewildering pieces, drawing impossible architecture designs that excited the eye of the spectator.

Using Escher's work as inspiration, the team behind ustwo Games developed *Monument Valley*, a puzzle game for mobile devices where players cannot trust their own eyes. According to the game's press release, "*Monument Valley* is about discovery, perception and meaningful beauty."[73] The player's main task is to guide Princess Ida through a series of stunning settings, where what seem to be three-dimensional spaces are in fact created by impossible geometry and optical illusions. By sliding, turning and moving the settings around, new paths appear. The player knows it should be impossible to walk through them, but in this game where anything seems possible, these are the paths that take Ida to new locations and that move the narrative forward.

I play *Monument Valley*, and although one can finish this game in only one hour, I have been stretching it out for much longer simply because I am not ready to stop being amazed by the ever-changing landscapes and perspectives, the brilliant optical illusions and the constant creation of new realities. Within this game, architecture itself is a main character, and that's one of the reasons why it is so refreshing and novel. Another aspect is that violence is never needed to solve a puzzle. In an interview with *Ways We Work*, Ken Wong, lead designer at ustwo Games, observed that "we're at this stage in the evolution of games where we're understanding how we can offer more narratives. How to present other kinds of choices, and how to resolve conflicts in other ways, or how to setup conflicts to have resolutions other than violence."[74] *Monument Valley* presents us with intriguing conflicts that are solved through shifting our perspectives and thinking outside the box.

Furthermore, the team put a lot of work and effort into the visual aspects of the game. Each level was carefully designed so that every moment could be appreciated as a rich visual experience in itself, regardless of the gameplay. A player can activate a camera mode at any time in order to capture the artwork, which can then be saved or shared with other people. I think this is a very clever way to spread a message, which, in this case, is the game itself. Generally speaking, when people are surprised, they often have the urge to share it with others to see if they will have similar responses. By capitalizing on this behaviour, ustwo Games brings the game to a wider audience and demonstrates that forward-thinking games are suitable for everyone.

Although the feeling of surprise is a great way to captivate viewers, it is still a passing emotion. The astonishment felt by viewers upon seeing this kind of graphic piece will decrease as they become familiar with the novel aspects of the design. Nevertheless, as I established at the beginning of this chapter, surprise always gives rise to other emotions. As designers, we can think carefully about what new emotions we hope to spark, as well as how to keep the public engaged.

73 — ustwo Games. (2014). "ustwo ames launches the beautiful Monument Valley game for iPhone, iPad and iPod Touch," in ustwo Games press realease. London.

74 — Ways We Work. (2016). "Ken Wong. Lead Designer at ustwo Games and Monument Valley." Retrieved (September 3, 2018) from: http://wayswework.io/interviews/ken-wong-lead-designer-at-ustwo-games-and-monument-valley

DIE ZEIT

LE FIGARO

THE TIMES

Público

The New York Times

The New York Times

New perspectives

When something or someone makes us see things from a new perspective, it leaves a mark. If our perceptions are challenged, we may feel lost or even shocked, but we should also be happy to realize there are many different ways of seeing and interpreting the world. When a graphic design triggers a change in perspective, we will cherish it and remember it as something that really had an impact.

If we consider how we often face unusual or new perspectives in our own lives, it becomes easier to get an idea of the characteristics that a design should feature in order for it to have a similar sort of impact on viewers. Such an impact can be portrayed in design pieces that express innovation or that try to improve things. One thing is for sure, though. Transforming perspectives is not about sticking with what we know.

What is it that we know, then? Cultural truths, traditions and social conventions all fit into the category of what is known. Picture a regular morning where you have the usual breakfast and check out the morning news. Whether we're getting caught up by watching TV, reading a newspaper or scrolling through social media, we know that there will be news and that fresh content will be posted each day, each hour and even each minute. Bearing this in mind, Joseph Ernst, the founder of the London-based creative group Sideline Collective, created a project that provides an alternative and challenging take on this constant flow of information. The "Nothing in the News" project consisted of a collection of newspapers from around the world with nothing in them. No text, no images, no content, no news: just some placeholder blocks of colour and the newspaper's masthead.

The project's intentions were not to criticize journalism or minimize the importance of staying abreast of world events. In fact, Ernst argues that now more than ever newspapers play a vital role in modern democracies by sharing the truth. Nevertheless, the project attempts to interrupt information overload. It encourages the public to spend a few moments of our busy lives in silence and "to sit around and think. To switch off and be bored. To daydream."[75]

Maybe we don't need to be constantly alerted to what the world has to offer. Maybe it is okay to miss some social media notifications. By providing a place to breathe and enjoy silence in, "Nothing in the News" allows us to experience a moment of nothingness.

75 — Ernst, J. (2017). "Nothing in the News: Newspapers from around the world with nothing in them." Retrieved (April 20, 2014) from: http://www.josephernst.com/nitn.htm

Joseph Ernst: "Nothing in the News," 2017. Publishing project

Afterwards we are able to look at all of the information that is disseminated to us with a clear view, to understand it better and to make a conscious choice about the type and quantity of new data we want to consume.

Unfortunately, we are overwhelmed by more than news and social media. A multitude of brands also occupy our environment through unidirectional advertisements that allow us to do nothing but assimilate their presence. This is not the case for Motherbird, however. In a similar vein to Joseph Ernst's project, this Australian-based design studio found a way to look at brands from a new and refreshing angle that allows the audience to do the branding.

This approach was used for a branding project for Something, a creative agency from London. In reality, Motherbird found it only took one simple act to change how people look at and interact with logos. Taking advantage of the etymological meaning of the word *something*—"a certain undetermined or unspecified thing"—it replaced the wordmark with a blank that people could fill in themselves. As Motherbird's team explains, "The brand aims to challenge the way we view the logo by delving into the subconscious via the conscious. By censoring the logo and incorporating it into language we encourage the audience to fill in the gaps, placing Something™ in their mouths not just their eyes."[76]

76 — Motherbird Studio (2018). Something. Melbourne. Retrieved from https://www.instagram.com/p/BhOJvB2FCzq/

Taking the view that a brand is not merely its logo, Motherbird cleverly applied the same strategy to business cards, notepads and postcards. Although Something's brand name ultimately prevailed, I see this project as a reaction to the powerlessness felt by viewers when they are confronted by other logos. In some way, this "no logo logo" returns power to viewers by offering them an alternative way of reading branding material.

It can be really hard to change a bad habit or to stop a damaging practice. The principle of "New perspectives" may help to change the meaning of these habits and turn them into a medium through which new messages can surface. People tend to engage with messages that shake up our understandings of the world and deviate from what we previously took for granted. As designers, we are able to make this shift happen. Through graphic techniques, we can fight universally held truths and make society look at them in a new light.

Nick Hoskin will always wear ███████████™ **black.**

Creative Director
+44 (0)732 234 0843
nick@something.media
www.something.media

███████████™
to write about.

There's ████████ waiting inside.

E — hello@something.media
A — 2 Eastbourne Terrace,
London W2 6LG

Something™

Creative
Content
Agency

E — hello@something.media
A — 2 Eastbourne Terrace,
London W2 6LG

Statements

"Emotions are generated by judgements about the world."[77] All of us have beliefs about how things should be, and it is important for the preservation of our social structures to relate these beliefs to those held by other people. Therefore, designers shouldn't be afraid of expressing their own opinions about society and current events.

    Sometimes there are statements that may seem obvious, yet no one but the boldest designer has the courage to say them *out loud*. By using a strong graphic piece as an agent to exert an impact on society, designers can make people actively think about what is taking place in the world around them. If the target audience relates to the statements made in a design, the experience can elicit emotions such as admiration and may make people follow the designer's work more closely.

[77] — Desmet, P. *Op. cit.*

    For me, one such bold designer is Javier Jaén, whose editorial illustrations appear in magazines such as *The New Yorker, Time* and *National Geographic*, as well as in books published by Penguin Random House. His illustrations are a clear example of how much can be achieved with so little. Jaén deliberately uses metaphorical symbols to express the essence of an author's idea or point and to enhance the visual statement. His figurative and playful language makes his public think about what is being said and about what political or social subjects are being discussed. According to Jaén, "My opinions are in the form of an image; and because we are such visual beings, images have the advantage and the problem of being too syntactic, which makes it hard to express a more elaborate and broader opinion but easier to get to the point."

    Within the framework of print media such as magazines and newspapers, it is possible to find various articles that examine or critique a set of ideas, principles or beliefs and that scream for a strong visual interpretation. If we look at the example of *de Volkskrant*'s cover from 5 November 2016, what first appears to be a boxing glove turns out to be a "punching president"[78] through the intelligent use of colour and form. The glove works as a symbol of power that can hurt, leaving no doubts about the magazine's or Jaen's opinion on the United States' newly elected president.

    At this point, I would like to explore a side question: How can designers express personal opinions in their work when the client has opinions of their own? In discussing this question, Jaén explains that "obviously, work for a client is not 100% personal, but with time—as with every human relationship—

[78] — *Die Zeit*. (2016, November 23). Berlin.

Javier Jaén

Illustrator and graphic designer

What does emotional design mean to you?

As creators, I believe that it is important to notice what things make us emote and why we like them. What is it that caught our attention and interest? As creators, how we understand our emotions and also how we transform and apply them in our work are the things to take into account.

Your work is filled with political and social statements that can be seen as polemical. Was it a conscious decision to do projects on such topics?

When I think about it, I realize I didn't make any decision. As with other important things in my life, I didn't sit in a chair and think, "I want the world to know that . . ." I also don't see myself as a setter of public opinions or anything like that. Clearly, the images I design that appear in newspapers and magazines are just another tiny grain of sand in the public opinion. All of us have the desire to comment on current events—not just political events, but also ones related to our own lives: how we connect with others, how we change or how technology affects us, or even the new summer hit. We do it with our friends, with our partners or whoever. In my case, I also do it using my skills, although without any other reason besides the desire to comment.

Do you see your work as emotional?

I try my best so that my work is stimulating graphically and conceptually, preferably with challenging ideas in the background. If that elicits some kind of emotion or any reflection in that direction, great! I think the aesthetic and practical process is super important, but it is not my focus of interest, or what I get the most out of.

In my particular case, I'm not merely interested in producing beautiful work. I want my work to scratch, to hurt or to make an impact. I don't know if that is emotional, but as with any personal relationship, I want it to have a real effect on others.

Javier Jaén: "In Defense of Facts", 2016. Illustration

>

achtergrond
& opinie
# Vonk

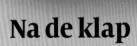

Na de klap

Of Trump nu wint of verliest, er zal geen reden zijn om
opgelucht adem te halen. Zijn campagne heeft
fundamentele ontwikkelingen aan de oppervlakte
gebracht die niet meer verdwijnen.

Illustratie Javier Jaén

you get closer to the people who you feel the most affinity with. Even at a professional level, little by little I've been building a network of clients (in this case mass media clients) with whom I am ethically and politically aligned. . . . With that in mind, I do feel that a major part of my work with mass media publications is personal."

What I take from Jaén's explanation is that it is important for there to be alignment between a company and a designer in terms of the core identity that they want to communicate—that is, who they are and what they stand for. Otherwise, the public will feel the inconsistencies and ignore the graphic piece itself.

Brussels-based poster designer Teresa Sdralevich managed to find this space for freedom when, after graduating from the University of Bologna, she found her way into the graphic design world. In her posters, she uses design as a weapon aimed at changing how people think. Addressing themes like sexism, the gender gap, the resurgence of Far Right politics, and economic and social rights through direct and impactful posters, Sdralevich has become an important figure in activist design.

She believes that "design is closely related to culture, democracy and communication, and uniting these is a question of designers' responsibility and self-awareness."[79] Sdralevich found a way to express her voice and opinion about our society by combining strong images and powerful slogans. With her designs, she invites members of that same society to reflect on and question their conduct and to take action.

If we believe that we have something important to communicate, we should do it right away. We can achieve this communication by using our work and by taking advantage of a brief or even doing it as a side project. We are

79 — Pelta, R. (2012, January). "Teresa Sdralevich: el cartel como cortocircuito visual," in *Monográfica*. Retrieved from: http://www.monografica.org/02/Artículo/3790)

creators, and we can use that fact to make people notice our ideas. As Javier Jaén puts it, creators "have a bigger mic or speaker," and they can use it to comment on current events.

Teresa Sdralevich: "Salaire égal," 2008. Poster design in the framework of the project "60/08 Let the walls speak"

>

À TRAVAIL ÉGAL,
SALAIRE ÉGAL !

-20%

who's afraid?

Designers can make their work come to life by expressing their freedom and creativity and not hiding their artistic side behind layers of technology. This will give projects a feeling of uniqueness and sincerity.

Design it

"A system which regards aesthetics as irrelevant, separates the artist from his product, makes mincemeat of the creative process—will diminish the product and the maker." —PAUL RAND

<

Expression

Can a graphic design piece be relaxed, annoyed, furious or excited? Can it have its own state of mind rather than representing the designer's or the audience's? Shapes, colours and typography all have the power to express pure artistic feelings that influence the mental state of the viewer and the creator. The simple movement or positioning of a line can express a lot about the overall emotional condition of the design. Consider an upward zigzag line, for example. It conveys a more energetic and ambitious feeling than a relaxed, soft, undulating line does. The same is true of colour. As I mentioned at the beginning of this book, the hue and saturation of a design's palette provide great ways to communicate different psychological features.

Whether in print or digital form, graphic design communicates meaning through its own inherent qualities. It is important for designers to be aware of and take advantage of this fact in order to improve communication with the audience. At this level, dynamic, improvisational, interactive and multidimensional approaches enrich the self-expression of the design and as a result encourage more natural and emotional connections with the public. If we examine our personal relationships, we can see that we tend to engage more with stimulating conversations than we do with monotonous and repetitive ones.

Speaking at the WebSummit 2016 in Lisbon, Pentagram partner Marina Willer pointed out that "being a designer in an ever-changing world means designing ever-changing identities and brands." The job of building rigid structures and guidelines with no margin for experimentation is outdated. Those guidelines wouldn't work in everyday life, where each day we face unexpected situations that remind us we don't have full control over our lives. So why should we impose them on design? As this Brazilian designer argues, we are art directors, not art dictators. Trying to impose too much order on our work is the first step to killing imagination and ending up with dull creations.

Creating flexible brands that adapt to their surroundings and evolve with their communities is a way to challenge these impositions. The Lyon-based creative agency Graphéine explored this idea when it was involved in the rebranding of the Saint-Étienne Opera House in 2015. The brief for the project communicated a desire to make the people of Saint-Étienne feel closer to and identify with this cultural venue. To fulfil this vision, Graphéine created a typographic logo that mimicked the building's architecture. Some of the typographic elements were then used to convey movement and

Graphéine: "Saint-Étienne Opera House," 2015–8. Visual identity and season campaigns

>

OPĚRA
SAINT-ÉTIENNE

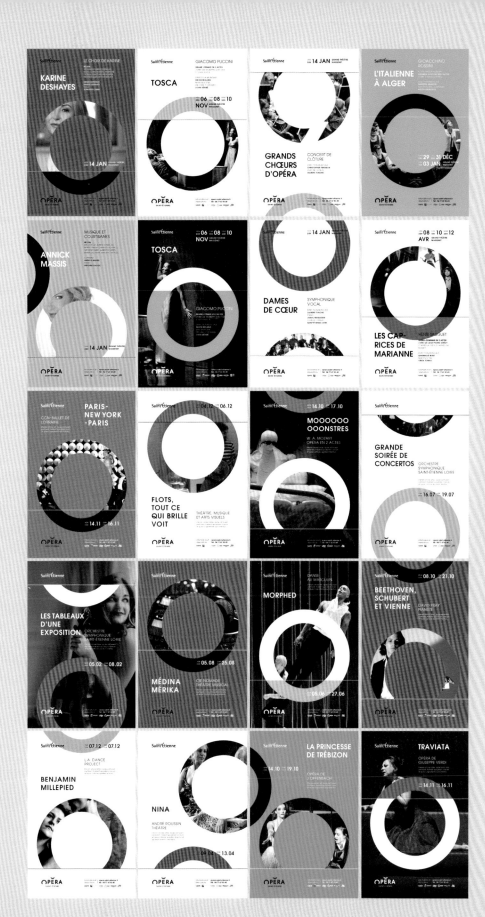

musicality on event posters, and some of them were used in a photographic series to showcase the opera house's personnel through their replacing parts of the staff members' smiles. The opera house's communication changes each season but is always recognizable due to its consistent and energetic visual language. Designers are currently faced with a challenge to "provide enough structure to guide exploration, but enough freedom to end up in unexpected and fresh places."[80] We shouldn't be afraid of experimentation and improvisation; these things bring visual identities to life so that they can express themselves and interact with the audience.

Running alongside the expression produced by the graphic elements, there's the designer's own expressiveness. As creators, we should sometimes be allowed to express our inner selves, our current identities. At times, a designer's self is so entwined with a piece that it becomes a key material in the piece's creation.

80 — Chimero, F. Op. cit.

As designers, being larger, louder and stronger brings us fans and cynics in equal measure. Both of these groups are provoked by powerful emotional responses that fulfil the most basic goal of graphic design: catching the public's attention. Chip Kidd, associate art director at Knopf in New York, spends his days designing book covers that are sometime praised and sometimes rejected, but never left unnoticed. Fulfilling his mantra that "all stories need a face," Kidd's covers are as expressive as they are seductive; they aim to give a good visual first impression of what the reader is about to get into.

But a first impression is not the only thing we get from Kidd's work in the case of his design for Haruki Murakami's novella *The Strange Library*. In this book, the designer also gives us a second impression—and a third and so on, until we finish the book and put it back on the shelf. Murakami's alluringly mysterious writing style is unmistakably personal, and so is the design created for this book. Striking images cropped from Kidd's Japanese advertising collection, bold closeups, bright colours and a lot of eyes looking back at the reader create the feeling that the book itself is telling the story. Both text and design allow the book to offer a unique reading experience that, in my opinion, wouldn't work as well if one of the two elements was missing. The design ends up being part of the story, and the images selected by Kidd illustrate the narrative so the reader "sees" it before reading the text.

At a TED talk in 2012, Chip Kidd said, "The book designer's responsibility is threefold: to the reader, to the publisher and, most of all, to the author."[81] In this case, Murakami couldn't have been happier with the result, stating to *The New Yorker* that Kidd's work always surprises him and that it "is one of the things that makes writing the books that much more fun."[82]

Designers are not brain surgeons, where being even a millimetre off can have severe repercussions on a patient. Our profession is important, of course, but the risks of doing it "wrong" don't have such severe consequences. So why not experiment a little? Through experimentation, we can find a style that both represents us as a person and effectively fulfils the briefings we receive.

81 — Kidd, C. (2012). "Designing books is no laughing matter. OK, it is." United States: TED.

82 — Kelts, R. (2014). "Illustrating Murakami." *The New Yorker.*

Make it for real

Revolutionary changes in computer technology have had a huge impact on the way in which we work and on how we plan our creative process. The development of computers' storage capacity and processing power has led to a growth in the number of design software programs that aim to make our jobs easier. Designers have become used to automated processes, the ease of using different approaches and the struggle for perfection that is an inherent part of working with such software.

This digital revolution has undoubtedly brought several advantages to graphic design, as we are now able to try different things in less time and without worrying too much about how a design will look in the end. However, this revolution has also made it easy for anyone to call themselves a designer. In fact, someone just needs a computer and an appropriate software program to create graphic design work. There is perhaps no need to point out that quality is often compromised due to a lack of knowledge about basic graphic design best practices. Cultural critic Johanna Drucker said something that I believe illustrates my point: "The tools of the designer are confused with the skills of the designer. . . . The accessibility of production tools has undercut the design profession since anyone could make a flier or a brochure."[83]

Although works created entirely on a computer have many merits and great value, their technological feel can sometimes be perceived as cold and distant. The conversation between designer and audience can get lost when a piece includes too many virtual components. These

83 — Drucker, J., & McVarish, E. (2009). *Graphic Design History: A Critical Guide.* Michigan: Pearson Prentice Hall.

Chip Kidd: *The Strange Library*, Haruki Murakami. Knopf, 2014. Book design

THE
STRANGE
LIBRARY

107

HARUKI
MURAKAMI

(1)

The library was even more hushed than usual.
My new leather shoes clacked against the gray linoleum. Their hard, dry sound was unlike my normal footsteps. Every time I get

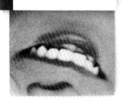

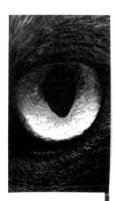

(12)

"Don't you have a voice?" I asked her.

"Destroyed?" I cried in surprise. "By whom?"
She didn't answer. Instead, she smiled sweetly. It was a smile of such beauty that the air seemed to thin around it.
"..................," she said.

"I understand," I said. "But

elements may make it hard for a viewer to appreciate that there's a person behind the graphics and not just a computer program or template. Today, there are even poster and logo generators available on the internet, making it even easier for anyone to design these pieces. On the other hand, if designers see themselves as craftspeople who create the graphic piece with their own hands—instead of relying on a computer's capabilities—the conversation might not only be more visible, but also more profound. By ditching technology and embracing handmade work, creators have the chance to showcase their formal design skills and to infuse their pieces with creativity, uniqueness, enthusiasm and passion.

To illustrate this principle, I would like to analyse the video game *Lumino City*, which was developed by the London-based studio State of Play. We can tell with just a glance that the game is different from others on the market. Looking closely at the background graphics, we can see that what is usually built using powerful 3D software is actually made out of paper, cardboard, miniature lights and small engines. When put together, these materials make the city look more natural and realistic. The camera movements of the game were filmed by its creators using a three-metre-tall model of Lumino's world, and the sound was recorded with a hands-on approach that matched the way in which the game was built.

There is a stark difference between digitally created projects that have a hand-crafted aesthetic and those that are actually hand crafted. In the case of the latter, the audience can sometimes see small errors that are characteristic of such projects, such as a bit of extra glue on one part or connecting wires on another. However, these details are what make the projects so real and charming. Returning to the example of *Lumino City*, players can almost feel the atmosphere of the studio where it was created and almost spot the fingerprints of the people who made it. "It was hard work but was worth it," says Luke Whittaker, one of the creators. "You get an effect which would be really hard to achieve otherwise—the lights cast a glow on the side of the building, and there's nothing uniform about them. I love the slight imperfections."[84]

84 — State of Play Games (2016). *The Making of Lumino City.* London: App Store.

Several reviews of the game state that although the game doesn't necessarily have the best user experience or game flow, people continue to play just to see more of the cardboard graphics. Players want to help Lumi, the main character, find her missing grandfather so that they can contemplate the game's awe-inspiring cinematography, which has been compared by some to a film by Wes Anderson or Laika Studios. The real value of this game lies not in the story itself but in the experience of constant discovery and in the delight of its settings. Even the game's creators were dazzled when they first saw the game images on screen: "It took my breath away a little. I was so excited by that, I thought 'if that just happened to me, maybe this can make others feel the same.'"[85] Designers can also experience this kind of enthusiasm from their audience by putting their hands to work, literally.

Sergio del Puerto and his Madrid-based creative agency Serial Cut provide another example of designers who use physical materials to create their pieces. Some of their advertising work for brands such as Nike, Microsoft, MTV, Cisco, IKEA and Toyota makes use of myriad objects that give the pieces a tactile feel.

85 — *Ibid.*

Sergio del Puerto has never considered himself to be a designer or illustrator, seeing himself instead as an image maker. Although these images are always retouched using 3D software, he believes that shooting on a physical set "makes the objects behave in a certain way when they are together: lighting, reflections and shadows give it a different look,"[86] in turn leaving the viewer in awe.

Unlike *Lumino City*'s backgrounds, no one can say for sure whether Serials Cut's final pieces have real objects in them. By retouch-

86 — Serial Cut. (2012). *ExtraBold.* (Sylvie Estrada, Ed.). Barcelona: Index Book.

ing digital components to give them realistic imperfections and overly retouching real components to make them look digital, Serial Cut teases viewers, making them wonder about what is real and what isn't. However, these ambiguous characteristics aren't accidental. The studio actually strives to pique its audience's curiosity and enjoys the fact that its projects create uncertainties among viewers and require people to spend more time looking at them.

Obviously, projects of this kind are time-consuming and difficult to create, which makes them a viable option only when there is time to experiment. It is similar to the process of writing to someone. Emails and text messages are, of course, faster and easier to send than written letters or postcards. But which of these ways of communicating are valued most in the long term?

Serial Cut: "Prius V," 2011. Campaign for Toyota USA

Projects that have the emotional satisfaction of the designer in mind—such as personal projects—are inspirational, motivational and educational, and they are vital for reminding graphic designers why they chose their profession.

Illumination

"Remember that the reason we do what we do, that we're carving our own path, is because we have a deep-rooted need to connect and this is how we do it." —ADAM J. KURTZ

‹

Stimulation

Advertising can (and probably should) have a social and cautionary role beyond its traditional call to consumption. Campaigns that attempt to affect how people and society as a whole act and behave should at some point be part of the communication strategy of every brand. After all, we are all responsible for the society we live in and should also all be responsible for improving it.

It may at times be difficult for designers to make clients understand that more can be conveyed through a graphic piece than just straightforward communication. In fact, an overly simplistic and direct message will likely end up becoming a design that only plays a minor role in the life of its audience. On the other hand, when designers create graphic pieces that help move people's stories forward, appeal to their attitudes and persuade them to alter their behaviours, truly emotional responses may be stimulated. In order to succeed in shifting behaviours and changing attitudes or beliefs, stimulation shouldn't mistakenly be understood as deception or coercion. It is better for shifts to come about voluntary so people don't feel as though they're being forced to change. How does one do this, though? First of all, it is important to convey credibility and desirability in a designer's work. People only change when they feel inclined to do so and when they believe this change will bring something better to their lives.

That being said, a message that amounts to "Don't do that! Do this!" should be avoided and replaced by a conversation with the audience. Designers can explain why the public should change, what the advantages of doing so are and how can we help them to be successful in this endeavour. The harder that change appears to be, the harder it will be for viewers to embrace it. This conversation will establish a relationship between the design and viewers, who as a result will feel more supported when it comes to their taking steps toward change.

Designers can make the process of change appear natural and effortless by showing steps toward the desired shift in behaviour and examples of how to achieve it. In the case of immense change, it is better to start the design campaign with one aspect of the change so that the transition from one attitude to another is smoother.

Imagine that someone wants to entirely overhaul the political system of a country. Where does graphic design fit in with such a project? The Swedish creative agency Snask had the idea of encouraging North Korea to transition from a dictatorship to a democracy. The motivation to change

Snask: "Love is Korea," 2016. Graphic identity

INFO

CAPITAL
Pyongyang
AREA
Total 120,540 km2 (98th)
Water (%) 4.87
POPULATION
2015 estimate   24,895,000 (48th)
2015 census   24,052,231[2]
DENSITY
198.3/km2 (63rd)
513.8/sq mi

20 ₩

500 ₩

obviously has to come from the country itself, but that doesn't mean Snask has to stand by and do nothing. They thus offered their help with what they do best: branding. After creating a complete rebranding campaign for the country—brandishing a message of love that was applied to everything from the flag to the national airline—the creative team sent an open letter to the North Korean embassy in Sweden offering their work for free.

The team knew that design itself wouldn't solve anything and that they wouldn't get an answer from its "client," but they did it anyway. As Snask's co-founder Fredrik Öst explains, "It's always been our dream project to do. Why? Because branding a country must be the most fun thing a designer can do." The studio also wanted to explore whether it could create any change at all with the help of design and branding: "We do think that you can make shifts in behaviour through graphic design but you need branding and politics," continues Öst. "You have to have something to say. Otherwise it's just pointless."

Speaking of politics, The American Institute of Graphic Arts (AIGA), which has the goal of "demonstrating the value of design by doing valuable things,"[87] launched the national Get Out The Vote campaign to motivate American people to vote in presidential and local elections. AIGA asked their members who are graphic designers to create nonpartisan posters that depicted the act of voting. Each poster was then showcased in an online gallery and distributed freely on the campaign's website alongside other assets and models that supported the campaign's message. "These political posters should be looked at as tools," says Laetitia Wolff, the campaign's curator. "Design has a real power to change behaviour."[88]

The campaign is part of AIGA's Design for Democracy programme, which is a collaboration between researchers, designers and policymakers who are committed to the public good. More than seven hundred designers have participated in the campaign, including big names from the American graphic design scene such as Paula Scher and Milton Glaser. They decided to put their clients' work to one side and try to bring about change by employing design and using their graphic skills to stimulate minds nationwide.

Some designers took a soft approach, while others screamed about the importance of voting to anyone who would listen. Whatever the strategy,

87 — AIGA. (2016). "Design for Democracy." Retrieved (September 11, 2017) from: http://www.aiga.org/aiga/content/why-design/design-for-democracy/design-for-democracy/

88 — Dawood, S. (2016, July). "AIGA Get Out The Vote poster campaign looks to activate U.S. voters," in *Design Week*. Retrieved from: https://www.designweek.co.uk/issues/4-10-july-2016/aiga-get-vote-poster-campaign-looks-activate-u-s-voters/

Fredrik Öst

Creative director, founder of Snask

I would like to start by asking, what "emotional design" means to you?

It's all about creating emotions with the help of design in all its forms.

Where did the idea of creating "Love is Korea" come from?

It's always been our dream project to do. Why? Firstly, because branding a country must be the most fun thing a designer can do. Secondly, North Korea would have massive challenges the day it became a democracy.

Regarding the letter to the North Korean embassy, did you have any kind of response from them? Did you expect any?

No, and we never expected them to. We did get threats, but none that we cared much about.

Did you make any other project with the goal of changing people's attitudes? Did it work? How did it make you feel?

Yeah, we did the feminist ten-year campaign Monkifesto for the fashion brand Monki. It was great and became a huge success around the globe. We felt great, of course. Every project that can actually make a difference is amazing.

Do you think big shifts in behaviour can be made through graphic design?

I'm not sure if you mean our project "Love Is Korea." We never expected it to actually change the country or create big debate. We simply wanted to investigate if we could create any change at all with the help of design and branding.

We do think that you can make shifts in behaviour through graphic design, but you need branding and politics. You have to have something to say. Otherwise it's just pointless.

How important is the role of graphic design in persuading our society to change for the better? What should a designer have in mind before starting a project with that goal?

Not mega important, but a message is sent and received. And the role of the designer is to make sure it makes this journey effectively and in a way that's as faithful to the sender's intention as possible.

Looking back on "Love is Korea," how do you feel about this project now?

We still think it's great and would do the same thing if we were asked today.

Matt Muñoz: (left) "Don't Vote...." 2016 / (right) Christine Wisnieski: "Vote America," 2016
Posters for AIGA's "Get Out the Vote" campaign

DON'T VOTE

UNLESS
YOU CARE ABOUT
THE FUTURE
OF

HUMAN RIGHTS · BUSINESS · THE ENVIRONMENT · FOREIGN POLICY · PUPPIES · RELIGIOUS LIBERTY · TRADE · SCIENCE · EQUALITY
ENERGY INDEPENDENCE · WOMEN'S HEALTH · THE AMERICAN DREAM · THE ECONOMY · THE PATRIOT ACT · EDUCATION
SUPREME COURT APPOINTMENTS · THE DEATH PENALTY · SOCIAL SECURITY · NICE THINGS · CLIMATE CHANGE · DRONE STRIKES
HANDLEBAR MUSTACHES · VOTING LAWS · LIFE · LIBERTY · THE PURSUIT OF HAPPINESS · BABIES · MONEY · IMMIGRATION
PRISON REFORM · GOVERNMENT SURVEILLANCE · KITTENS · CRIME RATES · WATER · HEALTH CARE · SELF-DRIVING CARS · CIVIL RIGHTS
TAXES · MARIJUANA · TACOS · DIVERSITY · FREEDOM · NUCLEAR WEAPONS · SPACE · TIGHTY WHITEYS · COMPUTERS · FARMERS
WELFARE · MINIMUM WAGE · SMUGGLING · GOVERNMENT REFORM · REFUGEES · INDEPENDENCE · THE INTERNET · PB&J · AIR
MEN'S HEALTH · FLUX CAPACITORS · JOBS · WALL STREET · FOOD TRUCKS · GUANTANAMO BAY · MUSICALS · THE DIGITAL DIVIDE
MILITARY SPENDING · TECHNOLOGY · FREE SPEECH · SUPERHERO MOVIES · PRESCRIPTION DRUGS · INTELLECTUAL PROPERTY
THE FEDERAL DEFICIT · INCOME DISTRIBUTION · THE CRIMINAL JUSTICE SYSTEM · OPPORTUNITY · CONSTRUCTION PAPER
PRIVACY AND DATE SECURITY · 'MERICA · YOUR MOM · YOUR DAD · YOUR FAMILY · YOUR LOVED ONES · YOUR COMMUNITY · EVERYONE

Vote America

the
professional
association
for
design

GET OUT THE VOTE
AIGA's civic engagement initiative, part of Design for Democracy.
Learn more: aiga.org/vote
Poster design by New Kind, Raleigh, North Carolina

V⊙TE411.ORG
In partnership with
the League of Women Voters

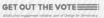

the
professional
association
for
design

GET OUT THE VOTE
AIGA's civic engagement initiative, part of Design for Democracy.
Learn more: aiga.org/vote
Poster design by studio of Christine Wisnieski, Cleveland, Ohio

V⊙TE411.ORG
In partnership with
the League of Women Voters

TO
VOTE
IS TO
EXIST

the
professional
association
for
design

GET OUT THE VOTE
AIGA's civic engagement initiative, part of Design for Democracy.
Learn more: aiga.org/vote
Poster design by Milton Glaser, New York, New York

V⊙TE411.ORG
In partnership with
the League of Women Voters

出來
投
票

the
professional
association
for
design

GET OUT THE VOTE
AIGA's civic engagement initiative, part of Design for Democracy.
Learn more: aiga.org/vote
Poster design by Jackson Fish Market, Seattle, Washington

V⊙TE411.ORG
In partnership with
the League of Women Voters

project or campaign, graphic design has the power to inform people about the pros and cons of certain conducts, make them think about their actions and possibly provide the extra push needed to change behaviours. And it feels good to be able to use design in this way.

Physical passion

You have to love what you do. I believe I speak for all of us when I say that we have all heard this message over and over again. There is a point to it, though. It is nearly impossible for projects that touch people's hearts to be created by a person who doesn't enjoy being a designer. People will more easily connect with our work if we put everything we've got into it.

Many design projects have been the result of the blood, sweat and tears poured into them, although usually not in a literal sense. Some designers, however, have chosen to show their commitment to and passion for their work by using their own body—as a canvas and as a design tool—to communicate their message. Although this approach may be shocking to some, it is also definitely emotional and impactful.

Perhaps one of the most controversial projects in this category is the poster designed by Stefan Sagmeister to advertise AIGA's 1999 talk in Detroit. It features typography carved in flesh, and according to the designer, the piece was an attempt to reflect the agonies of design work. By carving details of the event into his own torso, Sagmeister showed the design community that he is truly committed to the profession. Sagmeister believes that this project was a turning point in his profession, as he stopped worrying about digital perfection and started thinking about how to communicate his own personal mark as a designer. He also emphasizes that "it was indeed I myself who was involved, my doing, and hence my body. The image sprang directly from my chest, and its media success is proof enough of the impact such an approach has on the public."[89]

In a similar vein, the creative company Mother New York—in collaboration with the colour artist Stuart Semple and in celebration

89 — Hall, P. (2001). *Sagmeister: Made You Look*. London: Booth-Clibborn Editions.

of LGBTQ Pride Month—created a screen-printing ink made with the blood of its gay employees. This ink was then used to print one hundred limited-edition "Blood is Blood" t-shirts, which raised awareness about the practice of refusing blood donations based upon sexual orientation, which is backed by the American government and its Food and Drug Adminis-

Milton Glaser: (left) "To Vote is to Exist," 2016 / (right) Jenny Lam: "Voting Pictograms," 2016
Posters for AIGA's "Get Out the Vote" campaign

Stefan Sagmeister

Designer and art director, co-founder of Sagmeister & Walsh

Is it possible to touch somebody's heart with design?

I first started to think about this subject at the 1997 AIGA National Conference in New Orleans. Each and every one of us received a big black canvas bag, stuffed with goodies, conference programs, party invites and paper sample books, all designed by big-name designers especially for the big conference.

And it was all fluff. Well-produced, tongue-in-cheek, pretty fluff. Nothing that moved you, nothing that made you think. Some was informative but still all fluff. And there were tons of New Orleans clichés: jazz, striptease dancers, voodoo, crawfish, Mississippi steamboats.

Or combined clichés: jazzy striptease dancers performing voodoo on a crawfish while going down the Mississippi in a steamboat.

I think one reason for all this fluff is that we as designers don't really believe in much. We are not really into politics or religion and don't have much of a stand on any important issues. I guess when our conscience is so wishy-washy, so is our design.

I've seen movies that moved me, read books that changed my outlook on life and listened to numerous pieces of music that influenced my mood. Somehow, I never seem to be touched quite the same way by graphic design. I know, the comparison is not all that fair. After all, movies do have ninety minutes to do all that heart touching, and books have several days. Most graphic design has to connect in seconds.

How do you touch somebody's heart?

If I want to touch somebody's heart with a piece of design, it has to come from heart, it has to be true and sincere. Mere list following won't do. The audience of my design piece will feel if I'm honest, if it comes from my heart. Just like the way my friends know instinctively if I'm being authentic. If I'm true, if I have the guts, if I have the passion, my message will get through.

Then I thought: If I'm so eager to touch somebody's heart, why does it have to be with graphic design?

I mean: Why not touch somebody's heart by running a hospital in Calcutta? Why not write a really sweet letter to my mom?

Well, "How to Write a Sweet Letter to my Mom" does not sound like a particular interesting subject for an emotional desi talk. And I think that I'd like to touch somebody using a medium that I'm comfortable in.

Strangely, I also suspect that in ten years' time, this touching design is going to be the only kind of design that's going to be done by actual designers.

All that professional, good-looking, well-produced pretty fluff is going to be generated by sophisticated computer programs. You type in the client, select a format and a style, the program lets you choose from a vast list of visual clichés, downloads a picture selection, aligns everything and sends the file to the printer.

And I think I simply don't have the guts for the hospital in Calcutta.

Extracted from Hall, P. (2001). *Sagmeister: Made You Look*. London: Booth–Clibborn Editions.

Stefan Sagmeister: "AIGA Detroit," 1999. Poster

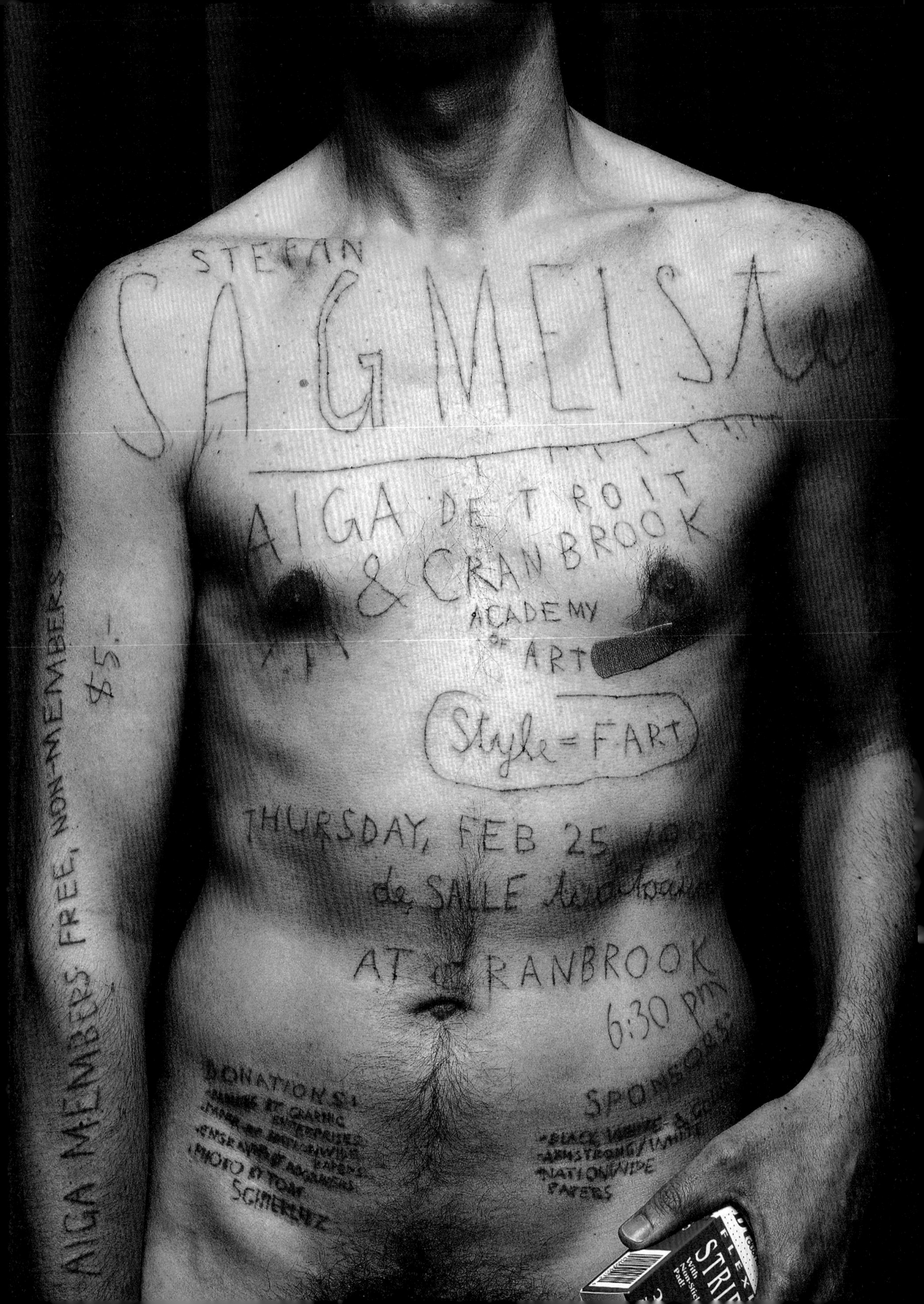

STEFAN
SAGMEISTER

AIGA DETROIT
& CRANBROOK
ACADEMY
OF ART

(Style = FART)

THURSDAY, FEB 25 199?
de SALLE auditorium
AT CRANBROOK
6:30 pm

DONATIONS:
CHAMPION GRAPHIC
MARK IT ENTERPRISES
MARK UP METALWIDE
JAMSKANDER PAPERS
PHOTO BY TOM
SCHIERLITZ

SPONSORS:
BLACK WHITE & GRAY
ARMSTRONG/WHITE
NATIONWIDE
PAPERS

AIGA MEMBERS FREE, NON-MEMBERS $5.-

THIS SHIRT IS PRINTED WITH
THE BLOOD OF GAY MEN.

THE BLOOD OF MEN WHO HAVE HAD SEX WITH MEN IS DEEMED
"TOO RISKY" TO DONATE. NOT BY SCIENCE. BUT BY THE FDA. BACKED
BY A GOVERNMENT UNWILLING TO REPEAL OUTDATED THINKING.
SEXUALITY IS NOT A RISK-FACTOR. STIGMA IS THE ONLY REAL RISK.

BLOOD IS BLOOD.

tration (FDA). The t-shirt design is entirely typographical and features a powerful slogan that reads, "This shirt is printed with the blood of gay men" on the front along with a further explanation on the back.

Since gay men can't donate their blood to hospitals—Reuters has estimated that the lives of more than 1.8 million people might be saved if they could—Mother's gay male employees decided to donate theirs to their own cause. Proceeds from sales of this shirt, which is being sold through The Phluid Project, are donated to the Callen-Lorde Community Health Center "to promote health education and wellness in the LGBTQ community."[90] This project received considerable media coverage, in part because of its bold statement but also due to the fact that designers used their own blood for their work as a mark of dedication to an admirable cause.

Clearly, it is impossible to follow the principle of "Physical passion" in every new project. First, we have to give our body a rest! Second, we

90 — Mother New York. (2018). "Blood Is Blood." Retrieved (June 16, 2018) from: http://bloodisbloodshirt.org/

should acknowledge that we won't please everyone. There is always going to be someone who won't identify with our work, whether this someone is the client or the audience. But there are others who will. Finding this particular audience will help to transform the message into meaning and appreciation. These are the people whom we should physically design for.

Uplifting experience

There are many different kinds of graphic designers out there. Some work for big corporations, others for small start-ups. Some open their own studios or even work as freelancers. Regardless of which category a given designer falls into, I like to believe that most of us became involved in the profession when we realised that this was our passion and that we could (and should) make a living from it. However, once this brilliant realization turns into everyday routine, it is easy to forget what brought us here in the first place. That shouldn't be the case. We should always be thinking about new ways to use graphic design beyond just promotion and advertising. Throughout this book, I have presented many dimensions of the importance of emotions in graphic design and ways in which feelings may be elicited from an audience, but a designer's own emotions are equally important and shouldn't be left aside.

In fact, the benefits of letting our creations trigger deep emotions within ourselves are huge, especially when one considers that a strong emotional connection will be established during the creative process and will be visible in the results. This connection is why undertaking personal projects is such an inspirational activity. Within them, we are our own bosses, and all the decisions will come from us. We can begin self-projects for a variety of reasons: to develop our skills in some area or technology that we don't usually work with; to make an idea that's been stuck in our heads for a long time come to life; or just to occupy our free time at the weekend. Whatever the reason, the ultimate intention should be to have fun and feel the *uplifting experience* of being a graphic designer without the rules imposed by clients' briefings and other people's expectations.

As a personal project based on a love for data visualization, Giorgia Lupi and Stefanie Posavec sent each other weekly postcards revealing details of their daily lives through data. Already working as designers in the field, they decided to undertake this project to fulfil a personal mission: rethinking data as a way to become more human and more connected to their inner selves. They called the project Dear Data, recalling a standard opening to a letter. Having met in person only twice, the two designers saw the project as the beginning of a conversation that would lead to a close friendship.

Each week, they set a different topic to gather data on. From how many doorways they crossed through to how many laughs they had or provoked, Giorgia and Stefanie would spend the week noting the occurrences and details of these actions. They later translated these notes into hand-drawn visualizations. While some weeks would reveal trivial facts about their lives, others would inspire deep emotions, such as the time when Stefanie felt homesick while looking at the visual representation of the hugs that she gave to her parents, or when Giorgia realized how many things she had been missing out on due to her insecurities. This project also created opportunities for personal discovery, as they developed valuable insights about themselves that allowed them to be better human beings. "We started Dear Data as a way to get know each other through our data, the material that is most familiar to us: but we soon found we were also becoming more in-tune with ourselves as we captured the life unfolding around us and sketched the hidden patterns we discovered in the details."[91] Personal projects will not only allow designers to enhance their overall practice but will also open them up to discovering and understanding more about their own personalities.

After the year of data gathering, Giorgia and Stefanie decided to share the results with the world through the creation of Dear Data's website. They did so in the hope

91 — Lupi, G., & Posavec, S. (2016). *Dear Data*. Penguin Random House.

Giorgia Lupi and Stefanie Posavec: "Dear Data," 2015. Set of postcards

66 Dear Data
WEEK 42: Laughters!

HOW TO READ IT:

this week I was in Italy, I tracked all of the laughters I had and I provoked, and noticed also the "big" ones I heard from others.

Each element is a [PERSON]:

Boyfriend
mum
dad
grandma
in-laws
grandma friends

Accurat, guys!

you!
(via txt)

friends in NY via txt!

friends in my hometown
ex boyfriend 😊
toddler 😊
others
(other people / not friends)

laughters provoked by someone else

laughters he/she provoked on someone else

= laughters he/she provoked on me
(the biggest = the biggest laughter)

= laughters I provoked in him/her

red dot = collective laughters

blue dot = it was a manifest joke

FROM:
GIULIA LUPI
BROOKLYN
- NY - USA

NEW YORK NY
30 JUN 2015 PM

SEND TO:

STEFANIE·POSAVEC

LONDON

· UK ·

ENGLAND

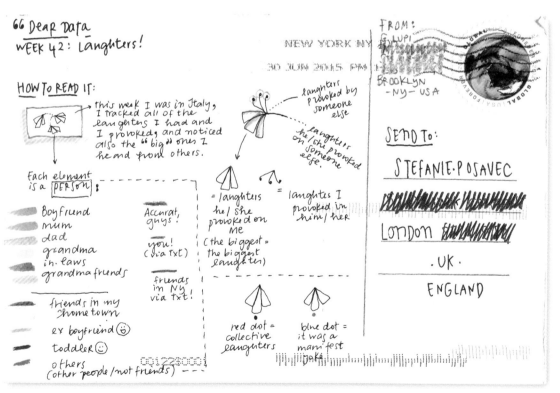

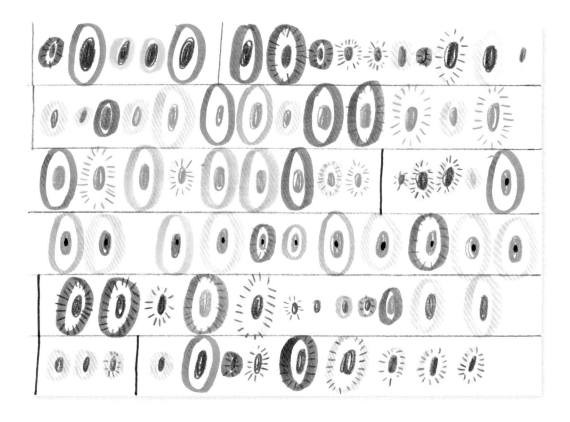

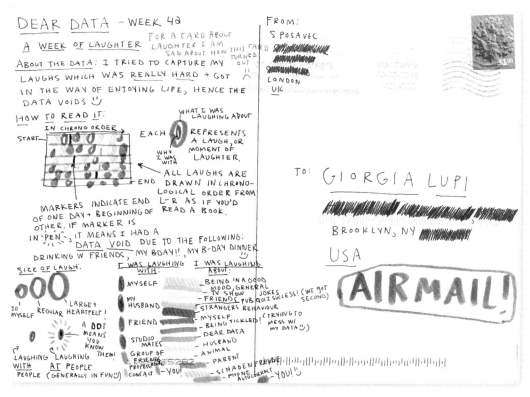

DEAR DATA – WEEK 42

A WEEK OF LAUGHTER

FOR A CARD ABOUT LAUGHTER I AM SAD ABOUT HOW THIS CARD TURNED OUT

ABOUT THE DATA: I TRIED TO CAPTURE MY LAUGHS WHICH WAS REALLY HARD + GOT IN THE WAY OF ENJOYING LIFE, HENCE THE DATA VOIDS :)

HOW TO READ IT:

IN CHRONO ORDER

START

END

WHAT I WAS LAUGHING ABOUT

WHO I WAS WITH

EACH REPRESENTS A LAUGH, OR MOMENT OF LAUGHTER.

ALL LAUGHS ARE DRAWN IN CHRONO-LOGICAL ORDER FROM L-R AS IF YOU'D READ A BOOK.

MARKERS INDICATE END OF ONE DAY + BEGINNING OF OTHER. IF MARKER IS IN PEN, IT MEANS I HAD A DATA VOID DUE TO THE FOLLOWING: DRINKING W FRIENDS, MY BDAY!!, MY B-DAY DINNER

SIZE OF LAUGH:

oOO

TO MYSELF · REGULAR · LARGE + HEARTFELT !

A DOT MEANS YOU KNOW THEM!

LAUGHING WITH PEOPLE (GENERALLY IN FUN :))

LAUGHING AT PEOPLE

I WAS LAUGHING WITH:
MYSELF
MY HUSBAND
FRIEND
STUDIO MATES
GROUP OF FRIENDS
PROFESSIONAL CONTACT
-YOU!

I WAS LAUGHING ABOUT:
– BEING IN A GOOD MOOD, GENERAL
– TV SHOW
– FRIENDS JOKES
– PUB QUIZ SUCCESS! (WE GOT SECOND)
– STRANGERS BEHAVIOUR
– MYSELF
– BEING TICKLED! (TRYING TO MESS W/ MY DATA :))
– DEAR DATA
– HUSBAND
– ANIMAL
– PARENT
– SCHADENFREUDE
– PHONE AUTOCORRECT
– YOU! :)

FROM:
S POSAVEC
~~~~~~~~~~
~~~~~~~~~~
~~~~~~~~~~
LONDON
UK

£1.00

TO: GIORGIA LUPI
~~~~~~~~~~~~~~~~
BROOKLYN, NY
USA

AIRMAIL!

that the initiative would inspire other people to develop creative projects out of mundane activities, and they also hoped to remind us to "slow down and appreciate the small details of your life, and to make connections with other people."[92]

    As Giorgia and Stefanie's example demon-strates, side projects can be simple. We just have to think about what we truly want to do—the reason why we became graphic designers in the first place—and do it. As the designer Tobias van Schneider pointed out in an interview about the importance of personal projects, "It's hard work. It's focused dedication at odd hours, trying new things, knowing every step of the way that chances of traditional success are slim. It's being fine with staying small."[93] Still, when we manage to push our creative boundaries to a level of transcendence, it will yield outstanding and passionate results. Ultimately, if we feel comfortable enough to share those results, the project may even touch other people and inspire them to create their own personal enterprises. Gratitude will come from these people and it will inspire us to put our hearts into what we do.

    I couldn't end this chapter—or this book, for that matter—without mentioning *12 Kinds of Kindness* by New York-based designers Jessica Walsh and Timothy Goodman. This was a year-long project in which the designers explored their personal behaviours in order to resist selfishness and to become kinder and more empathetic people. The project consisted of performing random acts of kindness such as trying to make commuters smile, telling their loved ones how important they were, or even asking people on the street what could they do to help. In short, all twelve of the experiments that Jessica and Tim tried had the purpose of "helping people, connecting with people, examining what it means to be human, trying to grow and evolve and using the creative process as a catalyst for that."[94]

    Although the project could be viewed as mere-ly a social or self-developmental experience, it also represents a way to use creative skills and design tools to support a cause bigger than the designer and to start dialogues that are needed by society. And as Jessica and Timothy suggest, "in many ways it is more meaningful than the cor-porate work."[95] In order to promote this experience and share the twelve steps to becoming kinder, Jessica and Tim created a diary-like website. Both believe social media should be used for good, and so they created

92 — *Ibid.*

93 — van Schneider, T. (2014). "Spotify's Design Lead on Why Side Projects Should Be Stupid," in *First Round Review*. Retrieved from: http://firstround.com/review/Spo-tifys-Design-Lead-on-Why-Side-Projects-Should-be-Stupid/

94 — Walsh, J., & Goodman, T. (2015). *12 Kinds of Kindness*. Retrieved (January 19, 2016) from: https://12kind-sofkindness.com/

Giorgia Lupi and Stefanie Posavec: "Dear Data," 2015. Set of postcards

‹

original artworks that could be shared by visitors to the site to promote even more acts of kindness.

95 — *Ibid.*

Graphic design is not a typical nine-to-five kind of job. We don't stop being designers once our clients' projects are done, and those same projects shouldn't be the only ones in which we invest our creative skills. *12 Kinds of Kindness* is a good example of how a simple idea for self-exploration can push the world forward in unimaginable directions. Projects like this can lead to more emotionally connected lives, inspirational insights and overall happiness, making them worthy of pursuit by every designer. However, as personal as the project may be, its significance lies in its impact. These projects are like gifts, and part of the joy comes from sharing them with others and letting them feel our passion. The world needs more gifts, more inspiration and more wonder: "We need wonder in order to keep moving and growing—to stay alive to the world. It gives us meaning and, in fact, makes us humans."[96] Let's create meaningful projects that remind us of why we chose to do what we do and of the impact that our work can have in the world.

96 — Bantjes, M. *Op. cit.*

Jessica Walsh and Timothy Goodman: "12 Kinds of Kindness," 2016. Art project, performance

TRUMP TOWER
BUILD KINDN
INSTEAD OF BUILDING WALLS, LET'S BUILD MORE KINDNESS AND MORE LOVE.

Final thoughts

It is clear to me that graphic designers should be concerned with and base their work on what is perhaps the most natural of all human traits: emotions. In fact, graphic design is a discipline made for people by people. Throughout this book, we have seen graphic design's great ability to inspire emotions. It would surely be unwise to not take advantage of that power. At the same time, I understand that it is much easier to talk about creating emotional design pieces than it is to actually create them. Emotions are felt in the brains of every single one of us, yet no one knows for sure if something that creates an emotional response in one person will trigger the same response in another individual. Thus, designers need to try to understand people, respect them and celebrate their different ideas, needs and lifestyles. This process is obviously easier to accomplish and more effective when the target population is small or is close to us in some way. The ability to use graphic design to touch the masses is something only a few designers are gifted with. And it also depends on the level of commitment a designer has to the project in front of them.

There is one final thought I would like to share. Nowadays, design is not the work of just a handful of people. Given that so many of us have access to a personal computer, an Internet connection and a few digital design tools, it is not surprising that more and more people decide to try their luck as graphic designers.

Nevertheless, having a computer is not the only prerequisite to being a graphic designer. This profession is not simply about choosing typefaces or picking the right colours, and nor is it merely about developing formal and technical skills. Being a designer is an attitude; it means cultivating a critical discourse about our work and being aware of what is being made all around the world. It is about constantly coming to terms with historic and current design practices and about having a say in how design could and should be done in the future. People notice this attitude; they notice good use of colours, the right choice of typefaces and a proper composition. However, there are times when people also notice something else: emotions. This happens when the concept behind the project transcends the project's technical execution and touches people's hearts, and it represents the moment when a good designer becomes an excellent one.

As designers, we spend most of our time in offices or at home working on some creative project. While we are sitting at our desks, we are also building emotional experiences that will create real human connections and will ultimately give life some meaning. I know this statement is a somewhat romanticized interpretation of what graphic design can do, but I do believe designers have the ability to play a great role in transforming

Jessica Walsh and Timothy Goodman: "12 Kinds of Kindness," 2016. Art project

>

DON'T BE AFRAID TO ACT FUCKING NICE

society. We can, to a certain extent, decide which emotions will guide our audience, meaning we are able to fill our world with positive feelings and actions. There is a famous phrase that says, "With great power comes great responsibility." In our case, there is a great social responsibility. It is our duty to wisely use the techniques outlined in this book and to ensure that our creations are aligned with a sustainable future for society as a whole. In the same way that we are able to guide people toward a more altruist, caring and compassionate way of living, we can also lead them down selfish, boastful or egocentric paths. As such, it has never been as important to cultivate an ethical and moral commitment in the creative community as it is now.

My hope is that more and more designers will begin to show empathy for their profession, their colleagues, their clients, their audiences and even the social context. In turn, more and more people will take notice and develop a taste for such pleasurable graphic communication. As the design educator Franc Nunoo-Quarcoo explains, "To appreciate and judge excellent design, we must live with it until its qualities, its meanings, sink deep into our conscious and subconscious mind, and if its appeal is deep and varied enough to be lasting, we can realize its excellence because our lives are being substantially enriched."[97]

97 — Nunoo-Quarcoo, F. *Op. cit.*

Design is a movement. It moves from the creator to the audience, and if people feel emotionally moved, they will pass it around and around until the work itself gains a life of its own. This is our way to shape the world according to our imagination. I like to think most of us became designers because we wanted to have this kind of influence in our communities and be a positive force for change. Fulfilling those ambitions means always trying to reinvent and surprise ourselves with new ideas and concepts. I would love to see where emotion-driven design can take us, and how big an impact such an approach could have in our future.

I would like to finish with this iconic statement: "Genius is one percent inspiration, ninety-nine percent perspiration."[98] An emotional graphic design is indeed a strong perspective on design that could positively change our society. The hard work required to achieve this type of design will undoubtedly be honourable. I believe graphic design at some point can become more important than the product it helps to promote. My proposal is that we, as designers, try to find room in the projects we work on (even the most commercial ones) to focus on the intellectual and emotional capability design has to touch people's heart.

98 — Spoken statement attributed to Thomas Alva Edison and published in *Harper's Monthly* (September 1932).

Adam J. Kurtz
www.adamjkurtz.com

Things Are What You Make of Them (2017), 116-117

Alex Trochut
www.alextrochut.com

"Time Out London: Brunch" (2015), 72
"Beautiful Decay, Issue T" (2008), 73

Brian Gartside with WATERisLIFE
www.briangartsi.de
www.waterislife.com

The Drinkable Book (2014), 45

Brosmind
www.brosmind.com

"Brosmind Criminals" (2013), 96
"Unicorn" (2009-13), 97

Camille Walala
www.camillewalala.com

"WALALA X PLAY" (2017), 100

Candy Chang
www.beforeidieproject.com

"Before I Die" (2011-7), 56-57

Chip Kidd
www.chipkidd.com

The Strange Library (2014), 148, 149

Christine Wisnieski
www.aiga.org/vote
www.christinewisnieski.com

"Vote America" (2016), 160

Claan
www.claan.com

"Signage and Wayfinding for Innovation Center" (2013), 124

Dejan Djuric with Leo Burnett Toronto
www.leoburnett.ca

"Printed by Somerset" (2016), 40-41

Domestic Data Streamers
www.domesticstreamers.com

"Data Strings" (2014), 104-105

Giorgia Lupi and Stefanie Posavec
www.dear-data.com

"Dear Data" (2015), 168-169

Google
www.material.io

"Material Design" (2014), 53

Graphéine
www.grapheine.com

"Saint-Étienne Opera House" (2015-8), 144-145

herraizsoto&co.
www.herraizsoto.com

"OmmWriter" (2010), 88-89

Hey Studio
www.heystudio.es

"Commentary – Berlin Exhibition" (2015), 17-21
"Arrels Barcelona" (2015), 20
"Jammy Yummy" (2014), 20

Intégral Ruedi Baur Paris and EO-Guidage
www.irb-paris.eu
www.eo-guidage.com

"Une gamme de signa-létique accessible" (2014), 120-121

Isidro Ferrer
www.isidroferrer.com

"Frida & Diego" (2008), 36
"12 Feria de Teatro en Aragón" (1998), 37

Javier Jaén
www.javierjaen.com

"In Defense of Facts" (2016), 136
Illustration for *de Volkskrant* (2016), 137

Jenny Lam
www.aiga.org/vote

"Voting Pictograms" (2016), 161

Jessica Walsh and Timothy Goodman
www.12kindsofkindness.com

"12 Kinds of Kindness" (2016), 172-173, 176

João Machado
www.joaomachado.com

"Construir Bauen" (2001), 24
"Oceanos" (1998), 24
"Cinanima" (2005), 25

Joseph Ernst
www.josephernst.com

"Nothing in the News" (2017), 128-129

Josef Müller-Brockmann

"5. Frühjahrskonzert der Tonhalle-Gesellschaft" (1953), 52

KresselsKramer
www.kesselskramer.com

"Hans Brinker Budget Hotel" (1996-), 76-77

Marian Bantjes
www.bantjes.com

I Wonder (2010), 29

Mathery Studio
www.mathery.it
www.offf.barcelona

"OFFF Barcelona" (2018), 108-109

Matt Dorfman
www.metalmother.com

The Psychopath Test (2012), 68
The Professor in the Cage (2015), 68
"The Elusive President" (2013), 69

Matt Muñoz
www.aiga.org/vote

"Don't Vote..." (2016), 160

Milton Glaser
www.aiga.org/vote
www.miltonglaser.com

"To Vote is to Exist" (2016), 161

Motherbird
www.motherbird.com.au

"Something" (2018), 132-133

Nuno Coelho
www.nunocoelho.net

"Compact Discothéque" (2003-7) 48-49

Oliviero Toscani
www.olivierotoscanistudio.com

"Hearts" (1996), 80-81

Paul Rand
www.paulrand.design

"Sources and Resources of 20th Century Design" (1966), 112
"Eye-Bee-M" (1981), 113

Serial Cut
www.serialcut.com

"Prius V" (2011), 152

ShaoLan
www.chineasy.com

"Chineasy" (2014), 92-93

Snask
www.snask.com
www.love-is-korea.com

"Love is Korea" (2016), 156-157

State of Play
www.stateofplaygames.com

"Lumino City" (2014), 153

Stefan Sagmeister
www.sagmeisterwalsh.com

"AIGA Detroit" (1999), 164

Teresa Sdralevich
www.teresasdralevich.net

"Salaire égal" (2008), 140
"Who's afraid" (2016), 141

**The Phluid Project
with Mother New York**
www.mothernewyork.com
www.thephluidproject.com

"Blood is Blood" (2018),
165

THIS is UMAMI
www.thisisumami.com

"#monologueando"
(2016), 99, 101

**Tom Haugomat and
DDB Paris**
www.behance.net/
    tomhaugomat
www.ddb.fr

"Volkswagen illustrated
campaign" (2015), 64-65

TRUE
www.trueart.biz

"Life Instructions"
(1994-2014), 60-61

ustwo Games
www.ustwogames.co.uk

"Monument Valley"
(2014), 125

Visual Editions
www.visual-editions.com

Composition No.1 (2011),
44
Tree of Codes (2010), 44

Walker
www.walker.ag

"Not here but now"
(2006), 84-85

Wolff Olins
www.wolffolins.com

"Zocdoc" (2016), 32-33

Yuta Takahashi
www.yutatakahashi.jp

Michael Debus:
*Erkenntnisweg und
Heiliger Geist* (2017), 28
Michael Debus: *Trinität
Special Edition* (2015), 28
Johannes Kühl, Johannes Greiner: *Anthroposophische Gesellschaft
und Freie Hochschule
für Geisteswissenschaft*
(2016), 28

17, 21, Courtesy Hey Studio
20, Courtesy Hey Studio.
    Photos: © Roc Canals
24-25, Courtesy João Machado
28, Courtesy Yuka Takahashi
29, Courtesy Marian Bantjes,
    Photo: © Sara Caldas
32-33, Courtesy Wolff Olins
36-37, Courtesy Isidro Ferrer
40-41, Courtesy Dejan Djuric
    with Leo Burnett Toronto.
    Photos: © Luis Albuquerque,
    Arash Moallemi
44, Courtesy Visual Editions.
    Photos: (above) © Sara
    De Bondt Studio; (below)
    © Universal Everything
45, Courtesy Brian Gartside
48-49, Courtesy Nuno Coelho.
    Photo: © Sara Caldas
52, © 2019. Digital Image,
    The Museum of Modern Art,
    New York/Scala, Florence
53, Photo: © Sara Caldas
56-57, Photos: © Candy
    Chang, Kristina Kassem
60-61, Courtesy TRUE
64-65, Courtesy Tom
    Haugomat. Art Direction:
    Raphael Ghisalberti
68-69, Courtesy Matt Dorfman
72-73, Courtesy Alex Trochut
76-77, Courtesy KesselsKramer
80-81, © 1996 Benetton Group
    - Photo: Oliviero Toscani
84-85, Courtesy walker.ag
88-89, © herraizsoto&co. 2017
92-93, © 2014 Chineasy Ltd.
96, © Brosmind 2013
97, © Brosmind 2013. Photo:
    © Meritxell Arjalaguer
100, Courtesy Camille Walala.
    Photo: © Charles Emmerson
101, Courtesy THIS is
    UMAMI; Creative Direction:
    Maider Mendaza and Adrià
    Rosell

104-105, Courtesy Domestic
    Data Streamers
108-109, Courtesy Mathery
    Studio and OFFF Barcelona
112, © 2019. Digital image,
    The Museum of Modern Art,
    New York / Scala, Florence
113, © 2019. Digital image,
    The Museum of Modern Art,
    New York/ Scala, Florence
116-117, Courtesy Adam J.
    Kurtz
120-121, © Intégral Ruedi
    Baur Paris y EO Guidage
    company. Photo: © Intégral
    Ruedi Baur
124, Courtesy Claan
125, © 2014 ustwo Games Ltd
128-129, Courtesy Joseph
    Ernst
132-133, Courtesy Motherbird
136-137, Courtesy Javier Jaén
140-141, Courtesy Teresa
    Sdralevich
144-145, Courtesy Graphéine
148-149, Courtesy Chip Kidd,
    Photos: © Sara Caldas
152, Courtesy Serial Cut,
    Photos: © Paloma Rincón
153, © State of Play Games Ltd
156-157, © SNASK x Asta
    Ostrovskaja
160, Courtesy AIGA
161, (left) Courtesy Milton
    Glaser; (right) Courtesy
    AIGA
164, Courtesy Sagmeister &
    Walsh. Creative Direction:
    Stefan Sagmeister. Photo:
    © Tom Schierlitz
165, Courtesy The Phluid
    Project
168-169, Courtesy Giorgia
    Lupi and Stefanie Posavec
172-173, 176, Courtesy
    Sagmeister & Walsh.
    Creators/ Creative
    Directors: Jessica Walsh,
    Timothy Goodman

BERMAN, David B. (2009). *Do Good Design. How Designers Can Change the World.* (M. Nolan, M. S. Anderson, R. Berman, & S. Lysnes, Eds.) (1st ed.). Berkeley: New Riders.

BISQUERRA, Rafael (2015). *Universo de Emociones* (2nd ed.). Valencia: PalauGea.

BRADLEY, Heather (2015). *Design Funny: The Graphic Designer's Guide to Humor.* (Scott Francis, Ed.). Cincinnati: HOW Books.

CHIMERO, Franck (2012). *The Shape of Design.* (M. Brown, Ed.) (1st ed.). Minnesota: Shapco Printing.

DAMÁSIO, António R. (1995). *Descartes' Error: Emotion, Reason, and the Human Brain.* New York: Avon Books.

DESMET, Peter (2002). *Designing Emotions.* Delft: Delft University of Technology.

DESMET, P. M. A.; PORCELIJN, R.; & DIJK, M. B. (2007). "Emotional Design; Application of a Research-Based Design Approach," in *Knowledge, Technology & Policy*, No 20, 141–155.

HALL, Peter (2001). *Sagmeister: Made You Look.* London: Booth-Clibborn Editions.

HAVERKAMP, Michael (2013). *Synesthetic Design – Handbook for a Multisensory Approach.* Basel: Birkhäuser.

INNS, Tom (2007). *Designing for the 21st Century — Interdisciplinary Questions and Insights.* (Tom Inns, Ed.) (1st ed.). Hampshire: Gower Publishing Limited.

JORDAN, Patrick W. (2000). *Designing Pleasurable Products* (2nd ed.). Oxon: Taylor & Francis.

MÜLLER-BROCKMANN, Joseph (2003). *The Graphic Artist and his Design Problems.* Zürich: Verlag Niggli AG.

NORMAN, Donald A. (2004). *Emotional Design: Why We Love (or Hate) Everyday Things.* New York: Basic Books.

TOSCANI, Oliviero (1996). *Adiós a la Publicidad* (2nd ed.). Barcelona: Ediciones Omega, S.A.

RAND, Paul (1970). *Thoughts on Design* (3rd ed.). New York: Studio Vista/Van Nostrand Reinhold.

SAGMEISTER, Stefan (2008). *Things I Have Learned In My Life So Far.* New York: Abrams.

SAGMEISTER, Stefan (2012). *The Happy Film Pitchbook.* (A. Elms, Ed.). Philadelphia: Institute of Contemporary Art, Philadelphia.

WEINSCHENK, Susan M. (2011). *Diseño inteligente. 100 cosas sobre la gente que todo diseñador necesita saber.* Madrid: Anaya Multimedia.

VAN GORP, Trevor; ADAMS, Edie (2012). *Design for Emotion.* (Meg Dunkerley & Heather Scherer, Eds.). Waltham: Elsevier.

VICTORE, James (2010). *Victore or, Who Died and Made You Boss?* New York: Abrams.

WALTER, Aaron (2011). *Designing for Emotion.* New York: A Book Apart.

Sara Caldas is a Portuguese graphic designer based in Barcelona. After completing a bachelor's degree in communication design from the Faculty of Fine Arts at the University of Porto, she moved to Barcelona to enrol in a master's degree in communication design at Elisava. This wide set of influences sparked her interest in the theme of emotional design. She currently works as a UX/UI Designer at Citibeats, where she is helping develop the first empathetic artificial intelligence for cities.

Acknowledgements

First of all I would like to thank the school of Elisava, the place where this project started and where I got encouraged in my desire to write about design. A special thanks to Juan Arrausi and Jordi Cano—directors of the Master in Design and Communication—for their invaluable assistance; to David Lorente for mentoring the project, who was generous with his insights and feedback throughout the entire process; and to Albert Fuster—the school's Academic Director—for believing in this project and pushing it a few steps further.

Thanks to Joaquim Canet and all the Hoaki team for making this book a reality.

I would also like to express my gratitude to all the designers, studios, and companies who accepted participating in the production of this book for their significant contributions to its compilation.

To my friends and family, I appreciate all your efforts and continuous support. A special thanks to the ones who read my words countless times and helped me making sense of my thoughts.

To Teresa, Eduardo and Tomás, with love.